AF841823

Location of Production: Local vs. Global Game

LOCATION OF PRODUCTION: LOCAL VS. GLOBAL GAME

MIROSLAV N. JOVANOVIĆ

Nova Science Publishers, Inc.
New York

LIBRARY OF CONGRESS CATALOGING-IN-PUBLICATION DATA

Available upon request

1-59454-616-9

Published by Nova Science Publishers, Inc. ✣ New York

CONTENTS

PREFACE[1]

Where economic activity will locate in the future is one of the most important questions in economics. Even though advances in technology have reduced the cost of transport, communication and information gathering and processing, hence curtailing the 'distance penalty', local proximity (clusters) of firms that produce similar, competing and/or related products together with supporting institutions still matter. Economies of scale, activity-specific backward and forward linkages (indivisible production), accumulated knowledge and skills, innovation, existence of sophisticated customers and a fall in transportation costs play relevant roles in the 'protection' of clusters and absolute locational advantages of certain locations. 'Global' competitiveness often depends on highly concentrated 'local' knowledge, capabilities and common tacit codes of behaviour which can be found in a geographical concentration (cluster) of firms.

JEL: F15, F23, R12
Keywords: global, local, cluster, linkages, history, lock-in.

---

[1] An earlier version of this chapter was published in the *Journal of Economic Integration* in 2003.

Chapter 1

INTRODUCTION

Does the eagle mount up at your command,
And make its nest on high?
Job 39:37

Where economic activity will locate in the future is one of the most important and challenging questions in economics. Progress in technology, changes in demand and moves towards a liberal economic policy create new challenges for theorists, policymakers and business executives. As a number of economic activities became 'footloose' and highly mobile, one of the most demanding and intricate questions in such a situation is where firms and industries would locate, re-locate or stay.

Any society and each market oriented firm must first refer to the problem of what, for whom, how and where to produce. With this spatial distribution of economic activity in mind, the purpose of this chapter is to contribute to the debate about the 'local' versus the 'global' location of industries and firms. The approach employed is conceptual: the objective is to clarify and explain key tendencies, rather than to provide definite answers to the issue of the influence and consequences between local and global spatial distribution of production.

The spatial location of a firm is an issue only in a situation with market imperfections. Without market imperfections such as distance, transport costs and uneven distribution of natural resources (so that the location matters), there are no problems regarding deciding on the location of production. Without market failures firms may break up into units of any size and operate in any location with no cost disadvantage.

The structure of this chapter is as follows. Following this introduction, part 2 outlines principal theories regarding the location of national and international firms. Part 3 discusses the controversial term and impact of globalisation. Part 4 considers issues linked with the location of firms and industries in specific geographical areas such as clusters. Light is shed on the role of history, chances, accidents and wars in the selection of certain places for the location of production of goods and services. The conclusion is in part 5 that 'global' competitiveness often depends on highly concentrated 'local' knowledge, capabilities and a common tacit code or codes of behaviour which can be found in a spatial concentration (cluster) of firms.

Chapter 2

THEORIES OF LOCATION

The study of the location of production (spatial economics) has a long, although somehow meagre history (Krugman, 1998, p. 7). In spite of the general interest, there is no consensus in the literature about the factors that influence the location of new businesses. The problem was noted, for example, by Ohlin who wrote that 'the theory of international trade is nothing but *internationale Standortslehre*' (teaching about international location) (Ohlin, 1933, p. 589). In the same vein, Isard wrote that 'location can not be explained without at the same time accounting for trade and trade cannot be explained without the simultaneous determination of locations. ...trade and location are the two sides of the same coin' (Isard, 1956, p. 207).

A country's or a region's level of income and it's structure of production (size, scope and variety of firms and industries) depend on at least two factors. The first includes a country's endowment of primary and derived stock of factors such as land, labour, capital, infrastructure, technology, as well as production, organisation and control skills and competences. The other element is how the country or region interacts with the external environment; in particular, the extent, level and form of its access to the international market for goods, services, capital and knowledge.

The creation of wealth used to depend in the distant past to a large extent on the local availability of natural resources. As the economy evolved, wealth creation started to depend more on physical assets (mainly equipment and finance). Prosperity of the modern economy and competitiveness of output depend not only on the physical, but also and increasingly on intangible assets such as knowledge, information processing, as well as on organisational and control potentials and capabilities.

Abundant natural resources may often be a problem for a country, not a benefit. A discovery of resources attracts gamblers, opportunists and crooks such as Francisco Pizzaro (Latin America), Robert Clive (East India Company) or Cecil Rhodes (South Africa). These resources provoke or contribute to civil wars: Angola, Congo or Nigeria. Elsewhere, abundant oil reserves and exports as is the case in Saudi Arabia, Bahrain or Kuwait keep local wages too high to permit the local development of the manufacturing industry. Foreigners from less well-off countries fill jobs in services in these countries. However, certain countries that are exceptionally poor in natural resources such as Switzerland, Austria or Japan are highly developed and amongst the wealthiest in the world. They base their prosperity on the most important resource: human capital.

Let us now turn to the principal theories of firm location. Realising the arbitrary character of our classification and its limits, we shall first look into the issue of how and where firms and industries locate in space without paying attention to the origin, control and ownership of the firm. Second, the issue of ownership and control is taken into consideration in order to get the full picture.

2.1 National Firm

A starting point in location (spatial) theory and economic geography is the national endowment of primary factors of production. *Adam Smith* and *David Ricardo* referred to the geography of production and spatial economics in an indirect way. A country specialises in the production of a good for which it has an absolute advantage in production. Hence, according to Smith, an *absolute advantage* determines the geographical location of production. Ricardo's argument is similar, but in his model a country specialises in the production of goods for which it has a *comparative advantage* in production. Regarding land, the fertile areas are put into cultivation first, while less productive land enters use only as demand for agricultural goods increases.

The models by Smith and Ricardo depend on constant returns to scale and on the assumption that competitive prices guide spatial resource allocation. Hence, free trade allows countries to gain, because they specialise in production that they carry out comparatively well. Such an assumption is challenged by the view that there are in reality important market distortions such as monopolies, externalities (pollution), controlled prices and rigid wages that do not tell the truth about social costs. As such, they send wrong price signals and may lead to the conclusion that trade liberalisation may make matters even worse! Thus some argued that protectionist policies were required for:

- the security of jobs, as was the case during the 1930s (and not only during this period), or
- the safeguard of infant industries, as during the 1950s, or
- rent shifting in oligopolistic markets, as during 1980s, or
- the safety of the environment, as is currently the case.

In addition to these classical models, in the standard neo-classical *factor endowment* or *Heckscher-Ohlin* model refers to locational fundamentals. The national endowment of factors (land, capital and labour) and their relative proportion decides the location of production. A relatively abundant national factor of production (compared with other factors) determines what a country produces and exports. Conversely, a country will import goods whose production requires factors that are scarce in the national economy. Considering cases of 'localisation' of industry in one or a few countries, Ohlin (1933, p. 133) simply argued that 'it must be shown that costs of production on the basis of existing factor prices are lower than in other countries: certain factors are cheaper here than abroad, which accounts for that condition'. In an empirical study of trade patterns of over a hundred economies, Leamer (1984) confirmed that the factor endowment model can explain these trade patterns rather well. This model elegantly assumes that there are no specific factors and that production functions are identical in all countries. As such, it does not give the answer to the whole issue, for it can not explain intra-industry trade. This type of trade (includes a large part of trade among developed countries) is not based on differences in factor endowments among countries.

The factor endowment model has been one of the two principal single-cause models in dealing with specialisation, trade and spatial location of production. The other approach takes account of differences in *technology, economies of scale* and learning by doing. It was conceived by Krugman (1979; 1980) and later developed and expanded both by him and by a host of others. In a nutshell, a variety of causes including history, expectations and changes in technology (not only factor endowment as before) influence a country's specialisation, geographical location of production and, hence, trade patterns. Differences in technology and increasing returns to scale change productivity levels. This in turn alters the bases for specialisation, spatial location of production and trade patterns. In the case where there are both increasing returns to scale and transport costs, there is an incentive to concentrate production. By spatially concentrating production near its largest market, a firm can both profit from economies of scale and minimise transportation costs. Economies of scale have a stronger impact on the location of modern, knowledge based production than was the case before the Industrial Revolution.

While one can not dispute the importance of factor proportions for the location of production and some processing of primary resources, this approach can not explain the location of footloose industry. In addition, this model does not consider market structure, economies of scale, demand conditions or trade costs. The Heckscher-Ohlin theory is not capable of explaining the location of an industry in regions with high mobility of factors such as the United States (US) or in countries with a broadly similar endowment of factors (France and Germany). A common feature in the standard trade theory is that it considers states, while it utterly ignores firm or regions, i.e. the distribution of economic activity within a country. This gap is filled by spatial economics.

In their survey of trade theory, Leamer and Levinsohn (1995, p. 1363) stated that 'one rather awkward assumption that cries out for change is that of equal numbers of commodities and factors. After all, we really don't know how to count either.' The existence of more goods than factors, trade costs and differences in technology present the principal obstacles for predicting the location of production and specialisation.

Harris (1954) argued that manufacturing firms tend to locate in places where they have favourable access to the market. He showed that the industrialised US regions were also the areas of high *market potential* (a large market attracts producers). The idea is that firms choose to locate in regions that have good market access. However, this access is good in areas in which many other firms exist and chose to settle. There is a self-reinforcing, snowball or herding effect in which the size of the market attracts still more firms. The underlining feature of this approach is, like in most models of spatial economics, that it is based on some kind of economies of scale that rely on a geographical concentration of certain production activities.

Countries tend to specialise and export goods for which they have a relatively large domestic market. It is this domestic demand or '*home market' effect* (Linder, 1961; Krugman, 1980) that induces production, rather than domestic factor endowment. The response by firms to strong local demand for a product is so powerful that it leads this country to export that product. Countries have a competitive edge in the production of these goods and thus gain an advantage in foreign markets, while they import goods demanded by a minority of the home population. The factor endowment or comparative advantage model would not predict the home market effect. However, economic geography would predict such effects. The US, Japan and Germany have the greatest comparative advantage in goods for which their home market is relatively big. These are standardised goods for mass consumption. Empirical investigation by Davis and Weinstein (2003) found support for the existence of home market effects, as well as for the role and importance of increasing returns in determining the production structure for the OECD.

At the heart of the location theory by von Thünen (1826) are differences in land rents and land uses. This model is primarily concerned with the *location of agricultural production*. While Ricardo focuses on the difference in the fertility of land, von Thünen studies how different agricultural lands around a city (marketplace) bid for various uses. The model assumes a given isolated city (one consuming centre) and surrounding agricultural hinterland, homogeneous land surface, free and costless mobility of labour and identical tastes at all income levels. Land rents are highest in the city. From there, they steadily decline to zero at the outermost limit of cultivation (beyond that limit, land is a free good). Hence the rent in a given location totals the difference between the value of its yield minus the sum of production and transport costs. Under the above assumptions the model explains the kind of crop that would be grown at places with different distances from the market. In other words, farmers decide on the type of production (dear to transport vegetables and cheap to transport grain) by taking into account land rent and cost of transport. As transport costs and yields differ among crops, the result is a spontaneous development of concentric circles of production around the city. Land is allocated among different crops in a (optimal) way that minimises production and transport costs of different crops.

Von Thünen's model is based on careful study of farming practices in northern Germany in the early 19th century. Such distribution of farmland is less obvious in the modern more intricate world, but there are certain remnants around large urban centres such as dairy production and gardening. This early model, however, does not consider the role played by economies of scale. There is no answer to the question if vegetables can be shipped in both directions: towards the city (in exchange for cloth) and outmost limits of cultivation (in exchange for grain). The model is, therefore, suitable for the analysis of a pre-railroad and a pre-industrial society.

The problem in von Thünen's model is to find which good to produce in the given location. In the optimal plant site model by Weber (1909) the branch of industry is given, so the problem is to get the spatial location for production. Weber's model takes the geographical location of markets, raw materials and population as given and assumes that there can be only one location for production. The objective of an individual producer is to *minimise the combined costs of production and delivery*. When the production costs are independent of location, the locational problem relates to the minimisation of transport costs for inputs and output.[1] This is the key condition in the decision-making process about the location of a firm. However, when there are key resources that are used on a large scale in certain industries and that are highly localised, this may affect the location of manufacturing industry. These industries would be attracted to locate near resource sites. Hence, this case is 'out of step' with the spatial uniformity and the underlying principle of central place location for some, but not for all kinds of manufacturing. The problem with this approach to the location of new firms is, however, that the initial, static locational needs of a firm may change over time as the firm, industry, technology, consumers' needs and tastes or markets change and develop. There is also a possibility for a historical accident which can be coupled with the economies of scale, lock-in effect and agglomeration.

Geographical remoteness can be a handy scapegoat to some, who may use it to explain why peripheral regions are marginalised in economic and certain social terms. Hummels (1999) argues that geographical factors remain an important determinant of both trade and location. He suggests furthermore that trade composition patterns and direct investment decisions can be sensitive to changes in the relative cost of different transport modes and information transfer. His proposition that international transportation costs have not declined significantly receives some support from Finger and Yeats (1976), who demonstrate that with the process of tariff liberalisation overseen by the GATT/WTO the effective rate of protection from transport costs exceeds that from tariff barriers for many commodities. It is, however, a shallow justification for many industries. Innovations in transport and communication technologies have made these costs rarely the most important determinant for the location of business. In addition, the cost of 'transport disadvantage' on exports is already included in the local factor prices. Hence, a peripheral location is not an insurmountable obstacle for a number of businesses as demonstrated in the cases of countries such as Japan, Australia, New Zealand, Finland or Ireland. Moses (1958) extended

[1] In the case with one market and two deposits of resources, the optimal firm location would fall inside the triangle area which links these three different spots.

Weber's work and integrated location theory with the theory of production. This allowed investigation of the relation between substitution of inputs and geographical location of a firm.

Christaller (1933) wanted to clarify and explain the rationale for the number, size and spatial distribution of cities. The analysis of this geographer is based on the idea of market threshold and transport distance. He put forward the idea that cities form a *hierarchy of central places*. This hinges on the supposition that larger cities can sustain a wider variety of activities relative to smaller (low order) cities and villages. Economies of scale are the source of such uneven distribution of production. The consequence of Christaller's model is that if there exist economies of scale, then the size of the market matters for the location of business. The concern is here, therefore, about the most 'national' product below which are other products. The hidden idea in this model is based on the minimisation of transport costs by rational consumers that make multi-purpose trips. In spite of its obvious value for the analysis of urban growth and distribution of services, this rigid application of the impact of market size neglects the consequences of unequal distribution of natural resources, changes in technology and negative externalities that come from agglomeration.

Developing the central-place theory and the issue of how the economy fits into space further, the economist Lösch (1940) started with a useful, but most unrealistic assumption, that there is a perfectly even distribution of raw materials and population. He starts his consideration of the economic landscape with a 'local' good and seeks to *minimise transport costs* for a given density of central places. In such a space, centres specialise in different products, hence there is a diversification of economic landscape. An efficient pattern of central places would have the shape of nested hexagonal (honeycomb) market areas with no empty corners.[2] This means that certain economic activities can be done only at a restricted number of locations. It was subsequently demonstrated that there is a wide range of geographical configurations of firms. The spatial arrangements that can satisfy the equilibrium condition include squares, rectangles and regular and irregular hexagons (Eaton and Lipsey, 1976, p. 91). Even though based on unrealistic

---

2 If one imagines a geometrically even distribution of centres across flat and homogeneous surface and the corresponding circles (representing ranges of goods) around them, then if one wants to cover all the space with circles, there would be an overlap between the two adjoining circles. If one draws a straight line between the points where the two adjoining circles intersect, one would get a hexagonal market space of identical size around each centre without empty corners, as consumers would purchase goods from cheapest (nearest) producer.

assumptions, the model of central places need not be easily disregarded. A coherent general equilibrium model found certain justification for the central-place theory (Krugman, 1993, p. 298).

While the background theory in Christaller's model of central places is implicit, Lösch's separate approach made it explicit. When they seek to find synchronised locations for many kinds of goods and services they use different arguments. Lösch's model is more becoming for the analysis of the manufacturing sector, while Christaller's hierarchies are more relevant for the tertiary sector (retail services). In any case, it appears that Christaller and Lösch deal with planning problems, rather than with considerations of market results.

The theory of central places points to the factors that need to be examined during the decision making process about the location of an industry or a firm. These factors are sources of supply, intersections of traffic routes and the centre of gravity.[3] In order to reduce inaccuracy in such 'technical' process (suitable for the centrally planned system) one needs to consider additional elements that are parts of a market based economy. They include actions of other functionally related firms, competitors, consumers and government policies.

The classical German location theory dealt with the locational decisions of firms which are in essence reduced to two issues: homogeneous distribution of natural resources over a flat space and optimum cost of transport. This literature was obsessed with the geometrical shape of market areas in an idealised landscape or with the optimal production site with given resources and markets. It ignored the crucial issue of market structure and competition. This was 'doing things in the wrong order, worrying about the details of a secondary problem before making progress in the main issue' (Krugman, 1992, p. 5). Organisational issues such as institutional reality and

[3] Paris and Madrid have relatively central geographical location in France and Spain, respectively. The same holds for Munich in Bavaria. In 1998 the capital of Kazakhstan was transferred from Almaty to Astana precisely because the latter city lies at the intersection point of major North-South and East-West transport routes. One of the reasons why Peugeot-Citroën announced in 2003 that it intends to invest and to locate a large (€700 million) car assembly factory in Slovakia (over alternative locations in Poland, the Czech Republic and Hungary) is that this country has good access to transport links and that it is 'in the centre of Europe' (*The Financial Times*, 15 January 2003). The factory would start production of around 300,000 small cars in 2006. The management intends to be closer to fast growing markets in the EU accession countries and to profit from wage rates that are a fifth of the rates paid in the EU(15) for similar industrial operations.

policies were put aside. Institution-free theoretical models avoid the problem of the impact of various policies on the location or reallocation of firms and industries.

Perroux (1950; 1955; 1961) introduced a predominantly intuitive concept of *growth poles* in spatial economics. The idea was discussed in the context of controversy between balanced and unbalanced regional growth during the 1950s. Geographical agglomeration, significant production linkages (with the key industry) and strong human contacts are necessary for the growth of a pole. A firm is located in a space consisting of poles. Each pole has both centrifugal and centripetal forces. Hence, each pole has its zone of influence (it attracts and repulses firms) and interacts with other poles. If, however, a certain pole does not have a degree of flexibility and adaptability to new technologies and changes in the market, it will stagnate and decline. For instance, France selected eight urban areas and bolstered their growth during the 1960s in the expectation that such policy would counteract the growth of Paris. Hence, the policy of geographical concentration of investments was diluted over time as it was coupled with political snags. Many other national 'areas' exerted pressure to be included in the select group of geographical poles for special treatment. The evaluation of the policy of geographical growth poles is beset by difficulties, as it was not vigorously implemented in practice.

Multiple equilibria create a situation for welfare ranking and set up many temptations to try to pick winners. The selection problem, however, remains unresolved, hence a *historical accident* (chance, arbitrariness) remains the unique deciding factor of the location. If governments want to tip markets towards a preferred solution, then it is timing and, to an extent, instruments that are crucial. There is only a narrow window of opportunity during which the policy may be effective. Otherwise, governments with their limited knowledge, instruments and resources try to stabilise artificially a 'naturally' unstable and evolving process.

Arthur (1989; 1990; 1994a and 1994b) argued that certain models of production geography give weight to differences in factor endowment, transport costs, rents and competition. In such case, the pattern of production locations is an equilibrium outcome. Hence, in these models history does not matter. The locational system is determinate and predictable (Arthur, 1994a, pp. 49-0). However, if one includes increasing returns and multiple equilibria into consideration, the new model has four properties that cause serious difficulties in analysis and policymaking. These features are (Arthur, 1989, pp. 116-7):

- *Multiple equilibria (non predictability)*: ex ante knowledge of firms' preferences and potentials of technologies may not be sufficient to predict the 'market outcome'. The outcome is indeterminate.[4]
- *Potential inefficiency*: increasing returns (*i*-activities) may uplift the development of technology with inferior long run aptitude.[5] Basically, a superior technology may have a bad luck in gaining early adherents. For example, the American nuclear industry is dominated by light-water reactors as a consequence of the adoption of such reactor to propel the first nuclear submarine in 1954. Engineering literature asserts, however, that gas-cooled reactor would have been a superior choice (Arthur, 1989, p. 126). If the claim by engineers is that Betamax is a technically superior system for video recorders, then the market choice of the VHS did not represent the best outcome. Similar arguments could be used for the triumph of DOS over Macintosh during the mid-1980s. In addition, the 'qwerty' arrangement for the typewriter keyboards was designed in the 19th century. Its name refers to the first six top line letters. Even though it has repeatedly been shown that this distribution of letters was suboptimal, the 'qwerty' system continues to be the standard for keyboards.
- *Inflexibility*: once an outcome such as a dominant technology begins to surface it turns out to be more 'locked in' and persist for a long period of time.
- *Path dependence (non-ergodicity)*:[6] small, unpredictable, random and arbitrary events (chances and accidents), path dependence and economies of scale in a non-ergodic system may set in motion mutations in economic structures and irreversibly decide the final

[4] Murphy *et al.* (1989) discuss multiple equilibria with respect to the process of industrialisation, postulating that a certain critical mass of industries may have to be involved in order for industrialisation to be successful. A parallel could be drawn with location theory, and a role for government policy to aid the 'take-off' of a particular location, and encourage firms to move to the location.

[5] Positive feedback economics may also find parallels in non-linear physics. For example, ferromagnetic materials consist of mutually reinforcing elements. Small perturbations, at critical times, influence which outcome is selected (bifurcation point), and the chosen outcome may have higher energy (that is, be less favourable) than other possible end states (Arthur, 1990, p. 99).

[6] An ergodic system (a pendulum, water in a glass) returns at the end to its original state, no matter the disturbances between the starting and ending points in time.

outcome. These events are neither normalised, nor averaged away, nor forgotten by the dynamics of the system.

In this model history matters, but the system's dynamics, increasing returns, multiple equilibria, lock-in effect and path dependence generate theoretical and practical limits to predicting the future spatial location of an industry with a high degree of certitude.

The probability of the location of an industry resulting from a historical accident is shown in highly stylised, graphical form in Figure 1. If the distribution of potential locations of an industry is concave (Figure 1a), with a single minimum and a corresponding single outcome, the location is not influenced by a historical chance. This type of distribution is exemplified by the mining and steel-making industries, which are normally located close to their source of raw materials. If, however, the distribution is convex (Figure 1b), with two minima, then there are two potential outcomes, each resulting in a different location which may depend on the historical chance. The third case represents a sphere in which there are *n* solutions for the location of footloose industries (Figure 1c). Hence, multiple equilibria make policy analysis conceptually difficult. This type of distribution is exemplified by corner shops, bakeries and petrol stations. However, firms in most industries need to be close to each other (i.e. they tend to agglomerate and create towns and cities), not only to be close to common suppliers of inputs, but also to foster competition and to facilitate exchange of information, which can be hampered if firms are spatially dispersed.

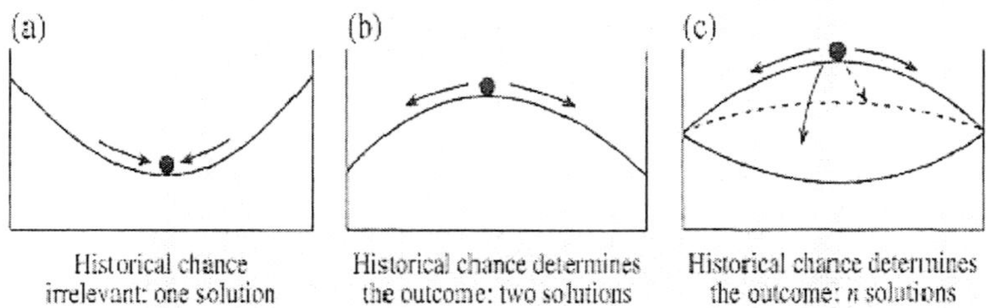

Figure 1. Concave (a), convex (b) and spherical (c) distributions of potential industry locations

Entrepreneurs (sometimes seen as 'maniacs with a vision') often have genuine ideas, but many of them do not have the necessary knowledge about how to run a business. Some of them may know, but cannot persuade those with funds to support their projects. Why is this so? Reasons include a number of cultural factors (risk lovers or risk averse investors) and the lack of knowledge and understanding to recognise and seize the opportunity. For example, a century ago a man went to a Belfast bank and asked for a loan to start a company. He explained to the bank managers that his invention was a mechanical horseless device that would replace horses in ploughing. This was too risky for the bank as it could not foresee that happening at all with a commercial success. Hence this man by the name of Ferguson went to Canada. He met another men by the name of Massey, they teamed up, and the rest of the story is generally known. Massey Ferguson became one of the major world producers of tractors and agriculture-related machinery. The moral of this story is that one needs to recognise and seize the opportunity at a critical time.

If agglomeration forces based on increasing returns are unbounded, then a single geographical location monopolises the industry. Which region is selected depends on its geographical attractiveness and the historical accident of firm entry, in particular early preferences of first entrants. If, however, agglomeration forces that come from increasing returns are bounded, then various regions may share the industry as if agglomeration economies are absent (Arthur, 1990a, p. 249). Locations with large number of firms cast an 'agglomeration shadow' in which little or no settlement takes place. This causes separation of an industry. Agglomeration occurs at a certain level of trade costs, while at another level of these costs, the spread of activities takes place. With bounded agglomeration economies, neighbouring locations cannot share the industry, but sufficiently separated regions can. In France, for example, Lyon lies between Paris and Marseille. Bounded agglomeration economies caused separation and dispersion. Again, 'which locations gain the industry and which become orphaned is a matter of historical accident' (Arthur, 1990a, p. 247).

2.2 International Firm

Ownership and control of the firm was neglected in the analysis by an implicit assumption that these do not matter or by the supposition that all assets are domestically owned. The presence of transnational corporations (TNCs) increases the mobility of capital, expands the availability of information and new products, changes competition structure and alters substitution of labour for capital. A TNC has different locational considerations than a comparable national firm engaged in the same type and scale of activity. A tendency is that strictly national firms expand where they already are, while TNCs enter where they think they may profit from access to the largest and growing market, favourable costs of labour, transport and/or taxes and subsidies. TNCs have 'organisational capital', i.e. a common set of rules, practices, routines and values which help them overcome various barriers while operating in different geographical, social, legal and other environments.

There are at least eight basic theories that explain certain aspects of why firms engage in trans-border business activities and become TNCs.[7] First, the motivation to control foreign firms may not come from the need to employ assets in a prudent way in foreign markets, but rather to remove competition from other enterprises. Hymer (1976) advocated such a *market-power* approach by TNCs. Reuber (1973, pp. 133-4) argued in a similar vein that long-term strategic factors for foreign direct investment (FDI) include the desire to eliminate competitors from foreign markets, to be within a protected foreign market, to secure low-cost source of supply and to lock the target country to a specific technology for a long time. Such a longer-term strategic view overshadows possible short-run variations in the profitability of FDI. The problem with this argument is that most of the TNCs (measured by their number) are small and medium sized. There were around 65,000 parent firms with around 850,000 foreign affiliates in 2002 (UNCTAD, 2002, p. 14). This shows that to become a TNC, a firm need not be a monopolist or an oligopolist at home and try to exercise that power abroad. If there is strong competition in the market for differentiated goods and services and if there is a high degree of substitutability between products (perfumes, soaps, watches, clothing, vehicles, passenger air transport on certain lines, to mention just a few examples), then the market-power argument for the transnationalisation of business is weakened.

Second, while the market-power model excludes potential rivals from competition, the *internalisation* theory holds that an arm's-length relation among individual firms is in some cases less efficient (e.g. trade in technology) than an intra-firm cooperative association. Profits may be maximised by means of an efficient and friendly intra-firm trade in intermediaries that eliminates sometimes excessive transaction costs (middlemen, exchange-rate risk, infringement of intellectual property rights, bargaining costs) which occur when the business is conducted through the market. In these circumstances a hierarchical organisation (an enterprise)

---

[7] In an early study, Weber (1909) offered two basic reasons why firms 'go to produce abroad'. The primary determinant is the achievement of lower labour and

may better reward parties in the longer term, as well as curb bargaining and incentives to cheat, than markets and external contractors. Payments of around 80 per cent of fees and royalties for technology 'take place between parent firms and their foreign affiliates' (UNCTAD, 1997, p. 20). This is an indication that TNCs play a key role in disseminating technology around the world (at least in the locations where they operate).

While Reuber and Hymer conceive TNCs as vehicles for reaping monopoly profits and for the internalisation of pecuniary externalities, the internalisation model looks at TNCs as a mode of business organisation that reduces transaction costs and internalises non-pecuniary externalities. This model of FDI may be convincing in some cases, but it may not explain the structure and location of all FDI flows. In addition to the internalisation possibilities, there ought to be ownership-specific and locational advantages for FDI.

Markusen (1984) tried to integrate TNCs into general-equilibrium trade models and locational patterns of firms that horizontally or vertically integrate across national borders. Intangible assets, as sources of multi-plant economies, are often firm-specific, rather than plant-specific. They include organisation, management, control, R&D, advertising, marketing and distribution. Many of these activities are centralised (finance) and present a 'joint input' across all production units. A TNC avoids replication of these activities that would be necessary if these units operated as independent national firms. This brings a 'technical' advantage to a TNC. However, if these advantages are transformed into market power, then the welfare effects of TNCs may not be clear.

Third, the *eclectic paradigm* (Dunning, 1988, pp. 42–5; 1999, pp. 1-3) explained the trans-border business activities of TNCs as a joint mix and interaction of three independent factors:

- In order to locate production abroad and be commercially successful, a TNC must have or control internationally mobile income-generating *ownership*-specific (O) advantages, assets, capabilities or skills. These firm-specific advantages include tangible and intangible advantages such as better technology, brand name, access to wide markets, monopoly, competence of managers, ability to innovate etc. that are superior to the ones that are available to local firms (including other TNCs) in the potential target country.

---

transport costs, while the secondary element is the benefit of large-scale production.

This is to say that a firm needs to operate either on a different production function than other firms or that it operates at a different point on the same function.

- *Locational* (L) (non-mobile) advantages refer to the comparative or location-specific advantages of the target country. They refer both to the geographical distribution of resources and to those created by the government.[8]
- There must be opportunities for the *internalisation* (I) of ownership-specific advantages (management and quality control, protection of property rights, avoidance of uncertainty of buyers, etc.). It should be in the interest of the firm to transfer these advantages abroad within its own organisation, rather than sell the right to use these advantages to other firms located in the country of intended production. Fixed exchange rates or a single international currency provide a degree of stability necessary for longer-term business planning with a high degree of confidence.

The eclectic paradigm claims that the exact mix of the OLI factors facing each potential investor depends on the specific context. If a firm possesses or controls ownership-specific advantages, then it may use licensing in order to penetrate foreign markets. If it has both ownership-specific and internalisation advantages, such an enterprise may use exports as a means of entering foreign markets. Only when a firm is able to take *simultaneous* return of OLI advantages, it will employ FDI as a means of locating and operating in foreign markets. This model, however, does not apply to diversified and vertically integrated TNCs (Caves, 1996, p. 5).

Fourth, the *product-cycle* model reasons that mature (and, perhaps, environmentally unsound) lines of production of goods (there is no explicit reference to services) are passed on to developing countries (Posner, 1961; Vernon, 1966). Such spatial reallocation of production is based on the experience of Anglo-Saxon firms and depends a lot on low factor costs.

The product-cycle argument as the major explanation for the location of business abroad and with a rather vague timetable for this spread of production can not pass the test of recent developments. Asian firms, however, do not replicate this pattern of location of production abroad on a

---

[8] For example, governments may change over a certain period of time the availability, quality and cost of the domestic factors. The disposable tools for this policy include training of labour and education of management, R&D, science, transport and communication infrastructure and tax policies.

large scale. The Japanese auto companies invest at home and in the US and Europe at about the same time for a similar type of production. There is a heavy concentration of FDI in developed countries (70 per cent of the world stock), while the majority of developing countries are relatively neglected in FDI flows. In addition, countries start investing abroad at a much earlier stage of their development than before. The newly industrialised countries and many other developing countries are investing abroad. In many cases these investments are in the developed world. Such developments may be prompted by the desires:

- to be present in the developed countries' markets (closer to wealthy customers)
- to be near the source and cluster of the principal technological developments in manufacturing, distribution, management and already existing infrastructure (to have a foreign 'listening and learning post')
- to participate in R&D programmes
- to avoid the dangers of protectionism in target countries
- to win public contracts
- to exploit the strength of host country's domestic currency

Fifth is the *follow your leader* hypothesis. Oligopolists are risk minimisers. They would like to protect their own market position and avoid destructive competition. Therefore, they typically try to minimise risk and follow each other into the new (foreign) markets (Knickerboker, 1973, p. 100). A study of timing of FDI by US TNCs in manufacturing seems to support this snowball or 'herd behaviour'. The Japanese TNCs in automotive and consumer electronic industries were 'following their domestic leader' when they located their manufacturing facilities in the EU and US during the 1980s and 1990s. This type of investment location behaviour is quite relevant during the opening phases of new markets. If a TNC has no previous experience in a certain new market, then the actions of competitors in that market may be quite informative. Examples of this 'herd behaviour' are the actions of TNCs in China and to an extent to eastern Europe at the start of 1990s. In addition, mergers and acquisitions 'mania' of 1990s in the EU and US shows how assets-seeking by one TNC may be followed by others.

Such 'catastrophic' relocation of industry as a result of the predicted behaviour of rival firms is one feature of the core-periphery model, one of the key new economic geography models. It is postulated that when trade costs lie in a certain range all firms in an industry may relocate *en masse*, although this would not be the optimum strategy for an individual firm were it to relocate on its alone.

While relatively low labour costs in China could have been the reason to start to locate certain operations there at the start of 1990s, things have changed. It was reported that China's Pearl river delta attracted $1 billion of FDI a month. Microwave ovens are produced in Shunde. Just one of its giant factories produces 40 per cent of global output of microwave ovens. Shenzhen produces 70 per cent of world's photocopiers and 80 per cent of artificial Christmas trees. Dongguan has 80,000 people working in a single factory making running shoes for the world's teenagers. Flextronics is a Singapore electronics maker that produces for Microsoft, Motorola, Dell and Sony. The manager of its Chinese plant in Doumen said that 'It is a myth that companies are coming here just for the cheap labour. It is the efficiency of the supply chain that drives them here as more and more of worldwide demand is consolidated in this area'.[9]

Sixth, the competitive international industry model for the location of business abroad refers to oligopolistic competition and rivalry within the same industry. This is basically *exchange of threats* (tit for tat strategy) to business moves by foreign rivals (Graham, 1978). Large firms keep an eye on the actions of their rivals, i.e., they act strategically (pay attention to the likely reaction of their competitors to their own actions). What Texaco does in Europe, Shell will (try to) do in the US. Competition is not 'cut-throat', but rather 'stable' among several oligopolies. Other examples of this rivalistic trend include FDI in the manufacturing of cars and tyres or supply of services such as hotels and advertising. Small and medium-sized enterprises (SMEs) such as gas stations in the middle of nowhere may in their business, act independently. However, SMEs in a cluster keep a vigilant eye on the actions of the competitors.

Seventh, is the *diversification of portfolios* model of foreign investment (Brainard and Tobin, 1992). This approach considers uncertainty. Fluctuations in the rates of return on capital invested in various countries introduce an element of risk. This inconvenience may be reduced by a diversification of portfolios.

Firm-specific assets and exchange rates may be the eighth basic reason for FDI. Suppose that there is a target firm in the US with an innovation (a

[9] J. Kynge and D. Roberts, 'The Pearl river delta is attracting $1bn of investment a month amid one of the fastest bursts of economic development in history', *The Financial Times*, 4 February 2003.

firm-specific asset) that can make the acquiring firm's assembly line 10 per cent more productive (10 per cent more output for the same level of input). If a US firm wants to acquire the target firm, then a change in the rate of exchange makes no difference as its gains will continue to be denominated in dollars. If, however, the acquiring firm is in Japan, the gains will be denominated in yens. A depreciation of the dollar relative to the yen will increase the Japanese firm's reservation bid, while the US firm's bid would remain unchanged. It is more likely that the Japanese firm would acquire the asset in this situation. The actual evidence about this taking place is rather mixed. The price of US assets needs not matter, only the rate of return: when the dollar depreciates, both the price of a US asset and its rate of return will go down. However, Blonigen (1997) found connection between exchange rate movements (weak dollar) and higher levels of Japanese acquisitions in the US in industries which involve firm-specific assets. This refers to the Japanese acquisitions in the US during 1975-92.

In addition to the above basic theories on why firms locate abroad, three other dimensions are relevant for coming to grips with the issue: cost minimisation, available technology and taxes. First, Kravis and Lipsey (1982, p. 222) argued that the location of foreign affiliates of TNCs is decided on the basis of *cost minimisation*. However, the intensity of this determinant varies from industry to industry. Second, Yamawaki (1993, pp. 19-20) did not dispute the importance of a relative difference in factor costs, the *availability of technology* in the target country is an additional and equally important factor for the location of Japanese FDI in the EU. A Japanese TNC from a certain industry decided to locate in the EU country which has a certain advantage over other EU countries in the same industry. Britain is preferred by the Japanese TNCs for the location of production of cars and electrical/electronic equipment, Germany for precision instruments and machinery, Belgium for stone, glass and clay products, while TNCs from the chemical industry prefer Germany, the Netherlands, Spain and France (Yamawaki, 1993).

Third come differences in *taxes and fiscal incentives*. While there are many 'tax havens' that attract quite a few firms (mainly from finance) and many countries offer different fiscal incentives to firms in order to attract them, is this enough by itself? Are tax incentives a bit more than 'corporate welfare'? Politicians use usually only three reasons to justify a local incentive programme. These three reasons are: jobs, jobs and jobs!

The importance, influence and evidence of taxes on the location of firms is still controversial. Investors may avoid locations that offer financial incentives as evidence of a region's non-competitiveness. Limited survey information reveal that fiscal variables matter little regarding business location. However, business executives often lobby hard for fiscal incentives. One can understand that attitude as firms have no incentives to forego such direct and indirect subsidies, even if they do not affect location decisions to a significant degree (Wasylenko, 1991). This was a confirmation of the results of an earlier study by Carlton which found that tax variables usually have a 'very small and always statistically insignificant' (Carlton, 1983, p. 447) impact on locational choice. Mody and Srinivasan (1998, p. 795) found that corporate tax rates do not have a major influence over FDI either by the American or by the Japanese TNCs.

A study into the effect of the elimination of a tax on paper for printing news (which accounted for about a half of the production costs) in the Netherlands in 1869 revealed that this assisted in the creation of new newspaper firms. Two thirds of these new entries took place in cities that already had other newspapers, while a third of new entries occurred in provincial towns that previously did not have a newspaper. Even though a cut in a weighty tax played an important role, the principal reason for this type of the location of firms was the size and growth of the local market. Hence, there is no basic difference in the rationale for a firm's location between a century and a half ago and now (Pfann and van Kranenburg, 2002).

Although many surveys give state and local taxes a low ranking on the list of location determinants, many locations in various states within the US can be close substitutes. In such a situation, even a small difference in production costs can play a key role for a particular decision about the location of business (Bartik, 1991, p. 8). As far as FDI by the American firms were concerned during 1984-92, they have become more sensitive to difference in host country taxes towards the end of that period (Altshuler *et al.* 1998).

This continues to be a controversial research area. There is a lack of consensus as the results of academic literature on the issue are still mixed. High(er) taxes may be preferred to low taxes by firms if the tax proceeds are used to finance local services useful for the business sector. In any case, high quality infrastructure is preferred by foreign investors to tax incentives. Transfer pricing and tax deductions in the home country provide other ways to minimise the tax burden on profit (Wheeler and Mody, 1992, pp. 71-2).

No single theory or model can provide a completely satisfactory answer to each issue related to trans-border investment activities of the firms. Motives for foreign production are different and they change over time in response to changes in the market, technology, tastes, management strategy, actions of rivals and economic policy. However, if taken together, these theories may provide useful elements for the understanding of the issue.

Chapter 3

GLOBALISATION

Liberalisation in the national and international economy is a policy choice of *governments*, primarily in the developed world. It is linked with privatisation and downsizing of the activities of the public sector and the expansion of the activities of the private sector. *Globalisation* of the economy and production is a fact. It is the outcome of the behaviour of *firms* (TNCs), their organisation, changing technology in production and distribution, control and finance, as well as economies of scale and takeovers. In part, it is also the consequence of a change in the behaviour of consumers (fickleness and declining loyalty to national producers and certain national products)[1] and liberalisation of national and international economies for trade, production and finance.

As a process primarily driven by technology and actions of TNCs (power is shifted from states to firms),[2] globalisation lacks two important

---

[1] One should not accord an absolute value to the decline of consumer loyalty to local brands. Regional, rather than 'global' strategies in certain food and health-care products may offer a superior business outcome. However, there was a certain 'global success' by, for example, Coca-Cola, which succeeded in replacing a part of the consumption of milk and healthy natural fruit juices for an artificial and sweet liquid that has a questionable impact on health and weight.

[2] It was the church that once determined our life, than the state and now it is corporations. Governments court firms (TNCs) to come and locate within the confines of their control. Critics say that the protection of the vulnerable in society or safeguarding of the environment is weakened, even that it is left at the mercy of big businesses. This may be the case in certain lines of production, but it all depends on specific circumstances. In some cases the regulatory framework facing TNCs was strengthened, while in others it was loosened.

components: transparency and accountability.[3] This process deals with the change in the geography of (integrated international) production and consumption as it reduces the importance of proximity to inputs or markets. It widens boundaries and deepens space for the geographical location of production and consumption because of the declining costs of getting goods and services to the market. A rapid expansion of FDI is the key component of this process. Capital market liberalisation and increased capital mobility have radically reduced the influence of governments in the monetary sphere. However, governments have gained increased control in other areas. For example, computers and information technology have greatly increased potential for data collection and processing, and consequently control over firms and citizens which is relevant for tax and other purposes.

Regionalisation is increasing in importance in the world economy. This was exemplified in the inability of 135 member countries of the WTO to agree even on the agenda for the 'Millennium Round' of global trade negotiations that took place in Seattle in 1999. Well-organised, vociferous and strong world-wide protests by environmentalists, farmers, enemies of genetically modified food and big business, labour unions, anti-capitalists and animal rights activists just added to the problems of that meeting and many others that followed worldwide. Therefore, the creation of integrated global economic policies is likely to be a very hard task for quite some time to come. It seems that the regional approach to economic problems will call the tune at least in the medium term.

The rapid international expansion of TNCs made them the most visible feature of globalisation. Being foreign, making sometimes visible and highly publicised mistakes and being often big, TNCs are easy targets for non-governmental organisations (NGOs) which can run successful campaigns to disgrace a mighty TNC. A number of NGOs are relatively small players who would like to 'punch above their weight' because of the urgency of the matter.[4] Examples of their campaigns include valid targets such as land

---

[3] The same holds for the increase in the power of special influence groups such as non-governmental organisations. Do these unelected groups of people with sometimes questionable accountability represent a risky shift of power towards special vested interests? Or do they represent a move towards the new 'civil society' (does anyone know the definition of this type of society)? Why does the general public believe sometimes more to these organisations that often lack resources for rigorous analysis than to the governments?

[4] NGOs often consider that it may be better to be just about right and make a big ado now in order to put an issue on the policy agenda, than to wait long for a firm scientific evidence and miss the political opportunity.

mines, HIV/Aids or poverty and third world debt. NGOs increased public awareness and pushed through agreements on the control of 'greenhouse gases' in the United Nations Conference on Environment and Development, the 'Earth Summit' in Rio de Janeiro in 1992. They also helped in torpedoing the Multilateral Agreement on Investment in 1998 and made a big ado in Seattle in 1999 (and many other subsequent meetings), which contributed to the failure to start a new WTO round of global trade negotiations before the meeting in Doha in 2001. No matter how justified the reasons for the campaign, these 'civil society' protestors against global capitalism demonstrated that the tide of globalisation could be checked and even turned back.

The anti-globalisation movement is moving beyond its radical, protest-driven even anarchist legacy (which might have worked against it) towards a movement with a concrete agenda. Rock-throwers, like Luddites (1811-16) that were smashing factory machines, were ineffectual and irrelevant in the long term. The strategy of the anti-globalisation movement is to address four weaknesses of the globalisation process:

- a lack of legitimacy,
- a lack of accountability,[5]
- a lack of organisation and
- a lack of transparency.

The idea is not to be against globalisation, but rather to put limits on it. The question is what kind of 'globalisation' is desirable and how to achieve it? The World Social Forum (Porto Alegre, Brazil) attempts hard to put under one umbrella hundreds of disparate groups. This Forum recommends a range of activities from limiting power of TNCs to adding new responsibilities and regulatory powers to the established international organisations such as the UN, the International Labour Office and the World Health Organisation. In this way the anti-globalisation movement may be able to gain more leverage on national and international scene.

The anti-globalisation campaigners have shown that governments are not powerless. The authorities can just as easily dismantle old trade and investment barriers, as they can introduce new ones. New technology, in

---

[5] The same holds for the increase in the influence of special influence groups such as NGOs. Do these unelected groups of people with sometimes questionable accountability represent a risky shift of power towards special vested interests or

particular the Internet, telecommunications, computing and data processing can offer some of the greatest economic opportunities ever for increasing living standards in all countries. Governments and the national elite in all countries (due to incompetence or indifference) have failed to explain this. However, the process needs to be coupled with balanced policies both in the rich and poor world. Even though global economic integration may be the best end point for the future of the world economy for the proponents of globalisation, it is more likely that other outcomes may be chosen for the time to come. Globalisation may be favourable for economic efficiency, but it can be harmful for social goals.

Apart from a partial integration of international production, globalisation brings risks and disruptions. Volatile capital flows, speculative attacks on currencies, financial crises and unpredictable reallocation of jobs are obvious examples of increased economic and social vulnerability of many countries, in particular in the developing world. To wrap up the issue, Henry Kissinger labelled globalisation as 'another name for the dominant role of the United States'.[6]

The vogue term 'globalisation' has not yet been well or clearly defined. Hence, this fuzzy, but powerful metaphor is overused; often abused and very often misleading. For some it basically refers to the choices and strategies, as well as the shape, extent, direction and significance of activities of TNCs. 'Globalisation has been defined in business schools as the production and distribution of products and services of a homogeneous type and quality on a worldwide basis. Simply put – providing the same output to countries everywhere' (Rugman and Hodgetts, 2001, p. 333).[7] 'Thanks' to al-Quaeda many realised that globalisation goes well beyond links that bind TNCs, producers, traders and bankers. For others, globalisation is linked with and invigorated by new technologies in communications and information processing. It is a sum of techniques that are at the disposal of private

causes? Or do they represent a move towards the new 'civil society' (does anyone know the definition of this type of society)?

[6] H. Kissinger, 'Globalisation: America's role for the millennium', *The Irish Independent*, 13 October 1999.

[7] Uniformity and homogeneity in the modern world may be a heavy price to pay for new or 'better' standardised things we consume. This introduces an ever present potential for the neo-communist danger that everyone eats and drinks the same, is dressed the same, uses homogeneous (perfectly substitutable) goods and services and ends up or is forced to, perhaps, even think 'the same'. If someone is not 'in step' with these global developments (no matter their democratic appearance and sugar-coating), well, then … the concerned may 'court trouble' from the central 'politburo'!

players and states. Yet for others, globalisation is an incentive to the reform process in economic strategy in many countries as outward-looking economic models replace inward-looking and TNC-hostile economic policy approaches. Others look at globalisation as a process that alters interactions among agents across space; still others equate globalisation with economic integration.[8]

The Internet symbolises the borderlessness brought about by globalisation. Physical presence in a specific location is not necessary. In the invisible continent of cyberspace, the users are 'everywhere and nowhere' at once. They use the Internet as a meeting place, a market, a distribution device, a library, and the like. This alters the geography of production, at least for certain products. Persons spend more time by working at home or 'on the road', hence certain office space (in congested cities) is vacated. However, one does not need to give an absolute value to globalisation. In spite of this process, localisation and clusters still matter. Firms that went furthest in 'globalisation' report that face-to-face contact is essential for the smooth organisation of business within the firm and marketing outside it. In addition, just try to tell that this is a 'borderless world' to someone that that wants to enter the EU or North America from outside. Borders continue to matter a great deal as people from different locations are prevented from crossing them without a cumbersome, costly and uncertain administrative procedure.

The Internet is based on communication and data that are located in computers that exist in the real world. Initially, this parallel universe of pure data existed everywhere freely in a 'lawless' world. The Internet was breaking barriers and eliminating physical distance. However, computers exist in an identifiable geographical space. If they can be located together with their users, then they are subject to law. Now governments are increasing their control over the cyberspace. For example, France prohibited the sale of Nazi memorabilia on the Internet; Iran banned access to immoral or anti-Iranian information; while South Korea prohibited access to gambling websites. There is also increased international police cooperation in combat against child pornography or computer viruses and hackers that attack major computer networks. Hence, borders are being created in the Internet. Even though the economic impact of geographical distance is being reduced, the local economic geography is keeping its strength.

[8] 'Globalisation is no more than an (admittedly ugly) name for the process of integration across frontiers of liberalising market economies at a time of rapidly

The imposition of 'global' standards may have its justification for relatively new and standardised goods and services such as copiers, fax machines, computers, mobile phones or better medicines, otherwise communication and exchange of information might be difficult and costly. However, the imposition of such standards for traditional goods (e.g., food) with the exception of health and the environment may not be easily justified. If needs and tastes for certain types of food are strongly locally specific (even the thickness of pizzas throughout Italy differs) why should one favour or impose global Pizza Hut type standards?

John Gray of the London School of Economics said that faith in globalisation melted down and that 'led by the United States, the world's richest states have acted on the assumption that people everywhere want to live as they do. As a result, they failed to recognise the deadly mixture of emotions - cultural resentment, the sense of injustice and a genuine rejection of western modernity - that lies behind the attacks on New York and Washington… The ideal of a universal civilisation is a recipe for unending conflict, and it is time it was given up'.[9] It is not that the people that live outside the Western world are unable to have liberal mind, rather there are social, cultural and institutional barriers that prevent a fast transfer of Western values, culture and institutions elsewhere. Then there are also 'recipients' choices. Do they really want and need what is exported or 'imposed' on them?

There was a faulty premise and vision that all people are culturally homogeneous that they think, act and most of all, shop alike (or like Americans); that there exist institutional bases for political democracy; and that the citizens are aware of their duties to one another and to the state. Checks and balances are mixed; there is mistrust vis-à-vis the government and state administration which has often deep roots in dictatorship, authoritarian and bureaucratic conduct, as well as in corruption. Without a very long term reform, education and trust-building, any attempt to transfer fast 'global' (social) standards would fail, and fail miserably, in many parts of the world. Lest it should be forgotten that 'it took 400 years for England to develop from that stage to its present one. To do the same elsewhere in half the time of 200 years would be a tremendous achievement; to aspire to

falling costs of transport and communications' (M. Wolf, *The Financial Times*, 3 October 2001, p. 15).

[9] *The Economist*, 29 September 2001, p. 14. The reference here is to the attacks of 11 September 2001.

do it in 25 or 50 years may be to court disaster' (Lipsey, 1992, p. 755).[10] There are stubborn local differences. Until the world becomes homogeneous, adaptation towards the local preferences and capabilities will be necessary. Problems regarding globalisation that appeared in the form of troubles regarding progress in the WTO or in the Multilateral Agreement on Investment illustrate signals of regional (triad: US, EU and Japan) or even local power.

It is true that the greatest and matchless advantage of free markets and globalisation is that they give free choice to consumers. Economic interactions are voluntary, so consumers are free to choose, for example, between local and global goods and services. But, this is only on the surface. If global products are advertised by large TNCs aggressively, including campaigns that are often beyond the financial capacity of local competitors, then the 'free choice' by consumers may be restricted and the local producers (and certain dimensions of the local culture) may be damaged. Critics of such unchecked global capital movements say that global TNCs put 'profits before people'. When these TNCs 'start talking about how they will no longer put profits first, people (rightly) think they are lying'.[11]

The critics of globalisation have certain valid points. 'The promise of export-led growth has failed in too many places. In particular, Latin America has signally failed to replicate Asia's success: Latin nations have liberalized, privatised and deregulated, with results ranging from disappointing (Mexico) to catastrophic (Argentina).'[12] In addition, India still remembers the moment when first ships of the East India Company arrived at the port of Surat. The Company came to India as a trader in 1608 and ended up virtually owing the country.

Another cost of globalisation can be found in the examples of countries such as Mexico, Thailand, Indonesia, South Korea and Russia. Globalisation

---

[10] Institutional elements such as clear property rights are very important for foreign investors. However, the mere transfer of these solutions from the developed countries elsewhere is not a sufficient condition for a successful economic performance. For example, while Russia has introduced a system of private property rights, China guarded the general socialist legal system. Nonetheless, domestic and foreign investors regarded China as a promising location for investment and this country became one of the prime locations for investment. There was a strong credibility that investments would be protected. In contrast, this credibility was lower in Russia in spite of the property rights system. Hence, this was one of the elements why Russia continued to score much lower than China as a location for investment.

[11] *The Economist*, 'A survey of globalisation', 29 September 2001, p. 4.

[12] P. Krugman, 'The Good News', *The New York Times*, 28 November 2003.

led these countries into financial crises in the second half of the 1990s. Without the exposure to global capital markets, the crises would not have developed as they did. The critics of this view argue that these countries would not have developed fast prior to crisis without such exposure. In any case, one ought to be fair and observe that certain 'global tendencies' were present in the past well before the current wave of globalisation. For example, there was (for whatever reason and means) a spread of certain European languages outside Europe; spread of Islam in Africa, Asia and Europe; or spread of Christianity in Latin America.

Trade and foreign investments (globalisation) are partners, not adversaries of social agendas, but they ought to be coupled with effective national and international institutions that ease adjustment problems (such as the polluter-pays principle). Globalisation may bring adjustment costs in the affected industries and labour markets, but this may be only transitory. The gradual opening up of markets in Japan during the 1970s, and later in south-east Asia during the 1980s and in China during the 1990s, demonstrates that as a country grows wealthier, it ceases to be competitive in the production of labour intensive goods. Such a country becomes an importer of these goods and concentrates its production on higher value-added activities.

Child labour, begging, theft and prostitution in poor countries would certainly decline if globalisation opened advanced countries' markets to the products made by their parents. Even though globalisation spreads symbols of highly dubious value such as Coca-Cola, McDonalds, MTV, Halloween or chewing gum,[13] it also spreads profound values such as the rights of women and children. However, it is unfortunate that this takes place at a much slower pace. A still unresolved problem is that under globalisation human rights may sometimes be more important than state sovereignty.

The debate about globalisation is often about jobs (social dimension). Supporters argue that it is beneficial and that it creates jobs, while critics argue the opposite and say that jobs migrate to trading partners and competitors. Certain segments of labour in all countries are suspicious of globalisation, as they no longer perceive the national government as a sure protector of their concerns against external threats. To counter these fears, the best long-term policy response may be to advance possibilities for education and training, as technical progress has a strong bias against unskilled workers.

---

[13] One thinks of the particular consequences of chewing gum for the cleanness of elevators and chairs.

As far as firms are concerned, there is the search by efficiency-seeking enterprises, particularly some TNCs, for seamless and wide international markets regarding trade and investment. On the one hand, the *globalisation* of economic activity is making national frontiers less divisive than was the case 'ever before'.[14] Such worldwide economic integration and integrated international production of goods and services whereby competitors are in each other's backyard are made possible by the expansion of information and telecommunication technologies.[15] That process is sometimes inverted, on the other hand, by the spread of *regionalism* pushed by relatively inefficient firms and governments that are driven by short-term election interests, even though the conditions for a relatively successful integration process, such as that in western Europe, may be largely absent.

Regional integration (a second best solution) may be a promising form of supranational governance in areas where there is a strong case for coordination and harmonisation of national policies. Integration may resolve conflicts through positive cooperation within a cosy group but, if pushed to the limit, it may undermine multilateral (first best) trade and investment systems and fragment the world economy into conflicting regional blocs. Regionalism and multilateralism (globalisation) need not necessarily conflict. If the regional blocs cooperate and if they adopt liberal external trade and investment policies, the outcome may be an overall welfare improvement. The pace of international trade liberalisation since the 1960s, as well as the extension of the GATT into new areas such as services and agriculture, might have been much slower in the absence of challenges posed by the progress in integration in the EU. The debate should not be between regionalism and multilateralism, but rather between liberalism and interventionism (Blackhurst and Henderson, 1993, p. 412).

It is often forgotten that the spirit of 'globalisation' does not bring anything essentially new. The need is for more freedom for trade in goods and services and for capital mobility (FDI). The economic role of national

---

14 Increased international mobility of factors, increased international intra-firm transactions, expanding international cooperative arrangements between firms, the increasing importance of knowledge, as well as a reduction in transport and communication costs, support the process of globalisation and are constituent parts of it. In these circumstances, individual actions of national governments may not increase global welfare (pollution is an example) and certain supranational rules may be necessary in order to deliver more beneficial outcomes.

15 Trade is relatively more concentrated within regions than FDI. This suggests that trade plays a more prominent role in intra-regional integration arrangements, while FDI has a greater influence on global integration (UNCTAD, 1993, p. 7).

frontiers declines as national economies merge in a single 'global' unit. In a nutshell, the idea is to return to the essentials of the system that was prevailing before 1914. Re-globalisation may be a more appropriate term.

An enlarged market is an important gain for efficiency-seeking firms in a small country. In a situation without integration, foreign countries can simply threaten a small country that they will introduce protectionist measures or 'sanctions' against it (frequent threats by the US to many countries). Such a warning can seriously undermine the quality of all economic decisions in a small country. Integration enhances and secures market access for partner countries, as well as increases the potential for long-term competitiveness of a small country's goods and services. A common market may eliminate or harmonise national incentives to foreign TNCs to locate in partner countries (which were previously subject to countervailing duties). It also mitigates non-economic considerations, such as political pressures on third country investors to locate in a particular country.

Transnational corporations behave like other firms: they primarily follow the opportunities for maximising profit while staying within the law. Size and growth of the local market, including privileged access to international markets (instead of mere differences in the cost of labour), are the most prominent motivators for their trans-border business operations. In addition, in a situation where market liberalisation became a widely accepted policy choice, there is an increase in the importance of created assets and structures (technology and ability to create it, business culture, capability to organise and control production and marketing, communications infrastructure, marketing networks) as determinants for FDI. Those are the reasons why 65 per cent of the activities of TNCs were located in developed market economies (measured by the stock of FDI in 2002) (UNCTAD, 2003). In spite of the talk about 'globalisation,' on average, a significant part of the output of affiliates is still sold on the local market.[16] In this situation the developing countries and those with the economy in transition face very tough competition to attract TNCs.

Foreign investors will locate their activities in a country that offers the most favourable mix of cost of operation (production and marketing), provided that this factors well into the longer-term vision about potential profit. FDI can be made simpler by regionalisation of the world economy

[16] 'Over 90 per cent of products produced in each of the triad regions is sold within that region. There is no global car. … well over 90 per cent of MNE manufacturing is intra-regional rather than global' (Rugman, 2002, p. 5).

and international economic integration. However, integration/regionalisation is only a supporting tool for the tendencies that bring globalisation of international business. Modern competitive firms are usually TNCs that 'globalise' their business in the search for seamless and widest markets. Therefore, an increasing share of domestic output even in the developed countries is under the control of foreign TNCs. The same holds for an increasing share of foreign output of domestic TNCs. Strong FDI relations may exist even though the countries or groups of countries are not formally integrated. Just take a look at the example of two-way FDI flows between the US and the EU.

Glue holding transatlantic relations together is not principally trade, but FDI. Large global interpenetration of FDI reduces the chance that regional arrangements may turn into closed blocs. A 'hostage population' of TNCs may reduce the fear of retaliatory measures. Extensive FDI links between the US and the EU helped reduce any potential conflict between the two partners regarding market access. The same is not yet true of Japan. There is a hope that Japan will mature as a foreign investor in future and that potential conflict with that country will be defused.

In order to avoid the weakening of the competitive position of EU firms in global markets, the EU may follow two courses, although there may be a strong appeal to employ a mix of the two. First, the EU may increase protection of domestic firms against foreign TNCs through measures such as rules of origin, local content requirements and other trade related investment measures. Second, the EU may open its domestic market and welcome foreign, in particular high-technology, TNCs to locate their manufacturing operations in the EU. As widely argued, EU firms in a sizeable part of its manufacturing industry are less efficient than their counterparts in the US and Japan. Suppose that the EU adopts a liberal economic policy; if the EU firms adjust and withstand competition from foreign TNCs, they may, in relative terms, gain more from market liberalisation than their foreign competitors.

A caveat for developing countries is that sometimes they use tariff proceeds for investment purposes. If that is the case, a customs union may dry up an important part of domestic investments by lowering tariff revenue. In a situation with many market imperfections, the opportunities for gains and losses are numerous. Hence, long-term gains in growth that originate in international economic integration may offset this loss of tariff revenue. However, the question asked by the public choice theory is: are we sure that the government of the day in a developing country cares or can afford to care about long-term gain?

Chapter 4

LOCALISATION

4.1 HISTORY AND EXPECTATIONS

a. Background

As already noted, the Heckscher-Ohlin theory is inadequate to provide the reason for the location of an industry in regions with high mobility of factors (US) or in the countries with broadly similar endowment of factors (France and Germany). Patterns of regional specialisation and location of firms and industries are often created by a historical accident. Ohlin noted that 'Chance plays a significant part in determining the localisation of industry… A different distribution of inventions would have caused a different localisation' (Ohlin, 1933, p. 137). More recently Krugman wrote: 'I at least am convinced that there is a strong arbitrary, accidental component to international specialization; but not everyone agrees, and the limitations of the data make a decisive test difficult' (Krugman, 1992, p. 9). In any case, chance and economies of scale are strong forces that influence the spatial location of firms.

When there are multiple equilibria, various spots for the location of business are substitutable ex ante ('putty'). After the investment is made, these locations can not be easily substitutable for quite some time ('clay'). Once a business is established at a specific geographical location, it is then 'locked in' through learning, path dependence, sunk costs, circular and cumulative causation effects (for examples of this putty-clay locational model). In this sense '…history matters in a way that it does not in neo-classical theory…' (Eaton and Lipsey, 1997, p. *xxv*). Two questions are relevant here:

- Are there inherent differences among locations that create predestination for certain activities?
- How can a small historical accident, a chance (something that is beyond the prior knowledge of an investor), alter the economic fate of an industry, region or a country?

Meaningful multiple equilibria exist when firms make independent profit-maximising decisions about output, prices and location. Sources of this multiplicity are pecuniary externalities that originate in (large) fixed costs and imperfect competition. The question is which equilibrium gets established? Will it be stable in the long-run? Since a particular space has only a limited influence on the location of new economic activity (especially footloose industries), what are the options for policy makers in this situation?

On the one hand, there is a belief that the choice is basically resolved by history. Past events set preconditions that move the economy from one steady state to another. This reasoning, found in the traditional literature, argues that history matters because of increasing returns and lumpiness (inseparability) and activity specific knowledge and capital goods (Eaton and Lipsey, 1997, pp. *x-xi*). The same idea is also behind promotional campaigns or 'location tournaments' (David, 1984) among countries to attract international footloose capital (TNCs). The idea is that once an activity starts in a place, it perpetuates itself and related businesses gravitate towards it. However, this 'self-reinforcing aspect of foreign investment begins to operate only after a certain development threshold has been reached' (Wheeler and Mody, 1992, p. 71). This is to say that spillovers on the local economy are not a direct consequence of the location of a TNC. Gains that come from these externalities can be achieved only if the local firms have, or can be motivated to take on, new (foreign) technologies and skills. The structure of the local economy, attitude of the private sector and policies of the government that promote change play a key role. In addition, there is evidence in the case of the US foreign investors that 'past investment in the country was a strong predictor of new investment. That persistence was attributed to the favourable effects of agglomeration' (Mody and Srinivasan, 1998, pp. 780-1).

There is, on the other hand, a view that the choice of equilibrium is determined by expectations. This observation is based on the belief 'that there is a decisive element of self-fulfilling prophecy' (Krugman, 1991, p. 652). Let us consider both views in turn.

b. Historical Lock-In Effect

The non-linear probability theory can predict with some certitude the behaviour of systems subject to increasing returns. Suppose that balls of different colour are added on a table. The probability that the next ball will have a specific colour depends on the current proportion of colours. Increasing returns occur when a red ball is more likely to be added when there is already a high proportion of red balls (Arthur, 1990, p. 98). Equilibrium depends on the initial point and latter arrivals. Hence, history as a series of (random) arrivals sets the final result.

The national rate of growth of capital stock (without FDI and foreign loans) depends on home savings and investment. Suppose now that one region/country initially accumulates more capital than the other does. In the following period both regions grow, but the one with more capital grows faster than the one with less capital. As manufacturing capital grows, the relative prices of manufacturing goods fall. After certain period of time, there is a point where the lagging region's industry can not compete internationally and it begins to shrink. Once this process begins the new theory of trade and strategic industrial policy suggests that nothing can stop agglomeration for a long time. Economies of scale may drive prices down in the capital-abundant region and at the same time the lagging region's manufacturing industry disappears. In this model, relatively small beginnings can have large and irreversible final consequences for the manufacturing structure of a country, its trade and competitiveness of its output (Krugman, 1990, pp. 99-100).

The dynamics of capital accumulation makes the region that starts with a higher capital stock than the other regions, end up with a dominant industrial position. If this is reinforced with a learning process and cumulative causation (strong internal production links where extension of one activity increases the profitability of others), than the existing pattern of comparative advantage is reinforced over time even if the overall structure of the economy has changed. This process-dependent development adds new layers of firms and industries on the inherited production structure. If output is concentrated within a relatively small spot, firms can benefit from economies of scale and linkages (growth of one activity increases the profitability of other). If this spot is close to a larger market, there are additional benefits in the form of lowered trade (including transport) costs. Hence, the current state of the economy determines its future shape.

The investment decisions and trade policy of a country in the current period will have an impact on the shape of the national economy in the future periods. For example, at the end of the 19th century Argentina and Sweden were relatively comparable backward farming-based economies. At about the same time, Argentina invested in the education of lawyers and priests, while Sweden invested in the education of engineers. The impact of such choice (coupled with other economic policies) on the material standard of living between the two countries is obvious.

Once the structure of an economy becomes unsustainable, there are certain critical branching points (bifurcations), at which the qualitative behaviour of the economy changes. New production geography either evolves or is triggered. This history dependent development can follow different paths, hence it is unpredictable. A long period of stability is broken up by an event of change (equilibrium is punctuated). For example, nearly all big cities are ports. However, it is a long time since New York or Boston ceased to be primarily harbour cities. One may find examples of punctuated equilibrium elsewhere. In biology, for instance, many species (crocodiles, crabs, turtles or monotreme animals) remain stagnant for a very long period of time. However, there are crucial, relatively brief and unpredictable moments (bifurcations) when new species arrive and old ones disappear. These include change in climate 64 million years ago caused by the fall of a meteor that provoked an enormous volcanic activity and fires, water and atmosphere were polluted, while smoke and dust prevented the penetration of heat from the Sun. Hence a very big part of life on Earth was frozen, burned, starved or suffocated. This change in climate caused the extinction of dinosaurs.[1]

More than a century ago Alfred Marshall spelled out the idea of 'backward-looking dynamics' or external economies (named in the modern jargon). In his analysis, factors of production are moving towards those industries in which they earn the highest current rate of return. If there are several meaningful equilibria in which the returns would be equalised, then the initial conditions determine the outcome. History matters together with factor endowment, tastes and technology (Krugman, 1991, pp. 653-4).

Marshall also described the concentration of specialised industries in particular localities in the following way. 'When an industry has once chosen a locality for itself, it is likely to stay there long: so great are the advantages which people following the same skilled trade get from near neighbourhood to one another. ... if one man starts a new idea it is taken up by others and combined with suggestions of their own; and thus becomes the source of yet

---

[1] One has to recall that dinosaurs probably came into being after an earlier fall of a meteor 251 million years ago.

more new ideas' (Marshall, 1890, p. 332). Contemporary jargon refers to these processes as externalities of innovation.[2]

Somehow similar 'first mover advantages' (to use the term from analysis of competition) may be found in biology as many bits and pieces of the past can be found long after their functions were lost. For example, 'embryonic birds and mammals still have gill arches, which have been useless for 400 million years. Why are the vestiges not eliminated by natural selection? The usual answer is that baupläne and the vestiges are developed early in the embryo and hence are most difficult to modify than features that develop later. The genetic programs controlling embryonic development were formed in the early days and have been frozen ever since' (Auyang, 1998, p. 195). A similar example can be found in the appendix in the human body. However, a question immediately comes to mind: why cannot newly created adaptive features be also frozen?

One of the chief causes for the localisation of industries can be found in physical conditions of the area. Metals producers located either near mines or close to sources of cheap energy. First-rate grit (for grindstones) was found near Sheffield, England, therefore it became the place for manufacturing of cutlery too. Another cause for the localisation of production has been the support of a court. In the Middle Ages many rulers in Europe have been constantly changing their residences (partly for sanitary reasons). They have frequently invited artisans from a distance and settled them in a group near the royal court. Once the court left, if the town survived, it continued the development of a specialised industry in many cases (Marshall, 1890, pp. 329-30).

Thus, cities often began to develop around royal courts and bishops' sees (concentration of consumers). Later on, the administrative, defence and educational dimension of towns and cities reinforced their function as consumers, but industrial production also started evolving in the cities. Today, many cities produce more value added than they consume.

Certain recent research provided some evidence that general government policy can indeed influence the location of firms and industries. Since 1947, a number of manufacturing industries in the US migrated to southern states because of the wish to escape unions. This was, however, only one of the reasons for the change in the location of certain business in the US. Others included innovation and change in transport (substitution of trucking for rail

---

[2] Because of the availability of wood, Sweden developed mighty pulp and paper industry. Strong links with the suppliers contributed to the replication of the success in the machinery that handles wood, pulp, making and drying paper.

which contributed to a spread in production), as well as the advent of air conditioning that 'made the climate in the South relatively more attractive than the climate in the North' (Holmes, 1998, p. 670).

Firms cluster together in order to benefit, among other reasons, from the availability of a close network of suppliers. They usually, but not necessarily, cluster in locations with large local demand. This demand will be large in the areas where most producers chose to locate (a process of circular interdependence or cumulative causation). 'There is a degree of indeterminacy in the location of activities – firms locate where they do because of the presence of other firms, not because of underlying characteristics of the location' (Venables, 1996, p. 57).[3] For example, there are around 600 tanneries in Arzignano (Vicenza, Italy), most of which employ just a few dozen workers. The region, however, produces 40 per cent of Europe's leather supply. The area around Vicenza does not only soak, dye, stretch, stamp, cut and ship material used for Gucci handbags, Louis Vuitton luggage, Nike sneakers and BMW car seats, but also produces gold chains, clothing and machine tools, many of them for exports. The major problem of a small or a medium-sized enterprise is often not in its 'smallness', but rather in its isolation which is eased in a cluster.

Should one in such an indeterminate situation search for answers to the questions on the geography of production elsewhere? Should it be outside standard economics? Should it be in non-linear dynamics (popularly known as chaos theory) which examines unstable behaviour with multiple dynamic equilibria, lock-in effects, bifurcations and extreme sensitivity to initial conditions; or in self-organisation (spontaneous appearance of order)[4] so common in complex systems; or in the new evolutionary economics[5] that has open frontiers, keeps an interdisciplinary dialogue and considers the role of

---

[3] 'Japanese business firms operating in Germany have an unexplainable attraction to Düseldorf rather than Frankfurt' (Beckmann, 1999, p. 61).

[4] Think of theatre when the audience applauds. After a brief period of time, it will all of a sudden start clapping at the same tempo without any conductor. Such self-organisation happens when many initially uncorrelated actions lock into each other's rhythm and create a strong collective group.

[5] Mainstream economics deals with decision-making within given structures. Evolutionary economics is concerned with decision-making and long-term changes of the structure. The interested reader is invited to consult a classical article on the issue by Boschma and Lambooy (1999).

history, technical change, institutions and development of human capital; or in evolutionary biology (evolution and hybridisation)[6] or elsewhere?

'Organisms are vulnerable, but they are not passive; they dig holes, build dams, modify the environment, and create their own niches of survival. Thus organisms and their environment interact, and together they form an ecological system that is better treated as a whole' (Auyang, 1998, p. 61). Similarly, the effects of externalisation are also pronounced in economics. Consumers' tastes and institutions, both public and private, interact, evolve and alter over time. Consumers, for example, in similar situations make different choices (recall the diversity of breakfast cereals, painkillers, cigarettes, chocolate bars, T-shirts, shoes, cars, cameras or bicycles). Hence, complex systems keep on moving from one pseudo-stable situation to another.

c. Expectations

Resources move gradually from one location and/or industry to another in response to differences in current earnings. If this shift is only gradual, then there must be certain barriers that increase the cost of the move. If there are costs, then the resource owners will be interested in expected returns in the future, rather than in current returns. However, future returns also depend on the decisions of owners of other factors and their expectations about future earnings. For instance, when a new technology is introduced, multiple equilibria cause expectations of potential action from competitors. In this model, expectations (rather than history) determine the future shape of the economy.

A river may, over centuries, bolster its bed and reinforce the work of natural forces over time. However, a strong earthquake (a bifurcation point) may instantaneously ruin such a long history. That was the case with the

---

6 Information in the physical world is transmitted via flows of particles such as electrons or photons and density gradients. In the social world (and to a lesser extent in the biological) 'there are the controls of information flows from the exercise of the *principle of optimum loss of detail* and use of *near-decomposability* within hierarchical structures - and even more so within the intricate interconnections of complicated hierarchical structures that may be embodied in an heterarchical model conceived by a human mind' (Isard, 1996, p. 357). Even though there are difficulties to apply biological analogies to social phenomena, they were widely used in the analysis of firms. The examples include the 'life cycle' theory of the firm, 'viability' of the firm and 'homeostasis' (habitual return to the initial equilibrium) (Penrose, 1952).

mechanical cash registers that were made obsolete by digital ones. Subsequently, optical scanners that read bar codes replaced digital cash registers. Those changes were all based on totally different technologies.

Other examples may be found in an almost overnight disappearance of the market for film cameras after the appearance of video cameras; the redressing of the market for mechanical watches after the invention of digital and quartz ones; a shift from dot matrix to bubble jet and laser printers; or fibre optics that evolved independently of the telecommunication technology. A good encyclopaedia has always been a must if the parents wanted their children well educated. A door-to-door salesman of Encyclopaedia Britannica has been replaced by Microsoft's cheap CD-ROM encyclopaedia Encarta produced first in 1993. In addition, Amazon is taking business from real world retail booksellers.

A new product (or service) has to be at least several times superior to the well established product, be it in convenience of use, price, size, shape and/or speed in order to remove the entrenched product from the market. No single source of advantage appears to last for very long. Even unique raw materials can be replaced by synthetic substitutes. Innovation is threatening firms from every side, hence the lock-in effect is not forever. High business concentration of a cluster/town on a single line of production can leave it highly vulnerable on external shifts in demand and technology. Rational entrepreneurs ought to treat bygones as bygones. Being a key player and staying on the top is not a state, but a process.[7] Hence, one needs to recall one of the main lessons from the two century long growth theory: it is innovation, rather than capital accumulation that is the real source of growth in the long term.

Even though they may be important, one may not wish to give an absolute value to external shocks. For example, the nuclear bombs dropped on Hiroshima and Nagasaki in 1945 had no long run impact on the size of these two cities. 'Within the space of just 20 years, they recovered from the devastation to return to their former place in the constellation of the cities' (Davies and Weinstein, 2002, p. 1283). Similarly, the impact of the bombardment of German cities during the Second World War on the city place in the economy and its growth was significant, but temporary

---

[7] Australians were stopped from selling their wines under French names such as champagne, chablis or claret. So they simply rebranded their products as sparkling wines, cabernet sauvignon and chardonnay. The French were subsequently forced to rebrand obscure labels with varietal names to compete with the Australians on the British market (*The Financial Times*, 28 July 2003).

(Brakman *et al.*, 2002, p. 28). There may be a stronger resilience to shocks in the locational fundamentals than one may expect a priori.

A clear example of how expectations shape the national geography of future production can be found if one considers the case of debt in the developing countries.[8] Back in the 1980s, these countries found themselves unable to repay huge debt owed to the big international banks. Had they all gone into default together, they threatened to damage or even sink the global economic system. The US Secretary of Treasury Nicholas Brady, developed a scheme for refinancing this debt, with the International Monetary Fund (IMF) playing the role of the financial policeman of developing countries by linking lines of credit to painful austerity programmes. This was taken to be a victory for the IMF and international institutions. It could have been, but only in the short run.

During the 1970s, the world saw a massive increase in the price of oil and other internationally traded commodities. The conventional wisdom (expectation) was that commodity prices would only go higher. The Club of Rome and other similar observers of history pointed out that the world was running out of scarce resources. The world was compared to a space ship: resources were being exhausted by growing populations and intensified industrial use. It followed that the price of commodities such as oil, copper and wheat could only increase. If this were the case, a rational expectation was that the best business area to invest in was in commodities. Correct?

The primary producers of commodities were developing countries that lacked manufacturing capability, but controlled natural resources so much demanded by the industrial world. Any sane investor in the 1970s knew that investing in industries that purchased raw materials was dumb, while investing in production of raw materials was smart. So everyone, particularly the international banking community and the World Bank, began investing billions of dollars into ventures designed to produce raw materials in developing countries such as Mexico over Nigeria to the Philippines. As the crucial commodity such as oil was expected to cost 40, 50 or even 100 dollars a barrel in the future, the cost of production was not a critical element in decision-making about investment. The price of commodities was going up and it was important to get into this business early. All of the technocrats simply knew this and the entire international economic system became skewed towards investing and lending to commodity producers in the developing countries.

---

[8] *Stratfor*, 'IMF's Camdessus misses the point', 15 November 1999.

As a consequence of the above process, the inevitable happened. It turned out that while the world may have a finite amount of oil or copper, there were still huge untapped reserves and progress in technology (which saves in the use of resources). When these megaprojects in the developing world started operating, the price of commodities collapsed. When prices fell below the cost of production, projects went bankrupt because of unsustainability. The outcome was the debt crisis. Nicholas Brady and the IMF stepped in to rectify the trouble. The debt crisis coming from beliefs in commodity scarcity led to an avalanche of investment decisions that has left a legacy of misery. The simplistic and linear projection of future in which commodity producers dominated industrial commodity consumers was rendered false by the collapse in commodity prices and made irrelevant by another phenomenon in the early 1980s. It is related to Microsoft and similar companies that came out of nowhere.

Microsoft, and the endless number of other software and related companies that appeared during the 1980s, altered the equation that had obsessed the World Bank and most other serious economic thinkers. The emergence of computing technologies and 'brain imports' in the US meant that it was possible to increase economic growth without having similar increase in commodity consumption. Microsoft and creators of ideas, after all, produce wealth without consuming commodities in proportion to growth.

A sharp increase in productivity[9] based on knowledge and innovation is in the core of the new economy. Investments by US firms in shorter-lived assets such as information and communication technology (supposedly important contributors to an increase in productivity) were very high during 1995-2000. After 2000, these investments shrank, but productivity growth accelerated. What is the reason for such type of growth? Are studies about productivity flawed? These studies may arbitrarily include or exclude depreciation. They may also assume that new computers have a direct impact and full impact on production from day one. In reality, however, it takes quite some time to master new equipment.[10] Or, are invisible and intangible activities such as formal and informal computer-related training and reorganisation of business methods more important than measurable investments in new equipment which show only tip of an iceberg? These

[9] Increased productivity (growth in output per hour) is the basis for an increase in living standard and economic progress in long term.

[10] The performance of computer chips doubles every 18 months (Moore's law). However, this does not mean that the impact of computers on productivity follows this trend in a linear way. It depends who, how, when and for what purpose uses computers: management of stocks or computer games.

intangible assets helped American companies produce more output with fewer production workers. As far as Europe is concerned, it had the worst performance in industries that are heavy users of information and communication technology, especially retail trade (where the US productivity is growing strongest which is obvious in retail chains such as Wal-Mart).[11] In addition, the US energy consumption in 1997 and 1998 was almost unchanged, while the US economy grew by 9 per cent during those two years.[12] Those economies that are successful in reducing energy consumption per unit of output can comparatively benefit a lot from increases in the price of energy in the future. The reason is that their competitors that have not done similar adjustments will suffer.

The extraordinary growth of the US economy has many causes. There is no doubt that the persistent growth of productivity in the US is due to the improvement in efficiency introduced by computing and 'brain imports'. Even Federal Reserve Chairman Alan Greenspan has acknowledged this, while also recognising that it is hard to calculate the impact. This much is apparent. At a time when productivity should be falling, inflation and interest rates soaring and the economy moving towards recession, growth in productivity (driven by the effects of computing, as well as new ideas) is keeping long term growth trend.

At the start of 1980s Japan produced cars and cameras at lower prices, smaller in size and better quality than the US. Two decades later the ability to produce cars, copiers and cameras is much less interesting than the ability to write software. The structure of production has shifted in a way that is almost beyond recognition. The hardware that runs a web server is much less valuable than the immaterial intellectual property that resides on the server. Perhaps the Japanese industrial targeting was superior during the age of fax machines, while the US liberal (unplanned) economic system and alert financial markets that force firms to adjust rapidly to shifting markets and changing technology are more becoming for the age of Internet (Krugman, 2000, p. 174). To put it bluntly, the Japanese bet on hardware, while the Americans bet on software. The decoupling of value from physical production, its shift to intellectual production, is a millennial shift whose full meaning will not unfold for many generations.

The firms that will define the next twenty years of economic history and production geography are probably completely unknown to anyone today.

---

[11] R. Gordon, 'America wins with a supermarket sweep', *The Financial Times*, 19 August 2003.

[12] *The Economist*, 19 August 2000, p. 9.

Uncertainty and risk are very high and the way forward is not always clear. Therefore, it is very difficult to know with high degree of confidence where is really going the world's economy. Deep changes that occur little by little (such as transformation in the economy and life that was brought by Microsoft) may be noticed only long after they happen. Therefore, the greatest danger is in 'linear thinking': the belief and expectation that what exists today will also exist tomorrow, but only with a higher degree of intensity.

The old industrial regions in advanced countries exhibited relatively long periods of growth. They were highly specialised in products that serve as basic inputs (coal, steel and chemicals) in the production of other goods or in the manufacture of goods for mass consumption (clothing or cars). However, competition from relatively low-labour cost Asian countries contributed to the economic decline of such clusters in the western countries from the 1970s. According to a dated model this process may find a parallel in the life cycle of a product. A more modern 'network' explanation adds to the economic aspects of over-specialisation a socio-cultural and institutional dimension to explain the meagre ability of old industrial clusters to learn, innovate, apply, absorb, spread and adjust to new realities (Boschma and Lambooy, 1999).

Technological, institutional and political lock-in in old agglomerations places the region in rigid trajectories. This path dependency, routine, a narrow focus on a specific activity and cosy relations between public authorities, business community and labour unions which safeguard the current structure, may often prevent the region from adjusting to new technologies and changes in demand, tastes and market situation. It is still not clear if dealing with such a situation calls for local institutional 'thickness' or 'thinness' in order to revive the local economy. There are at least two ways to address this problem:

- The neo-classical policy advice on this situation would be to enhance factor mobility.
- The evolutionary approach to counter this situation would be to increase local networking, learning and innovative capacity, to reduce dependence on various local 'lock-ins' and to stimulate new start-ups.

Even though there is a certain pessimism regarding the large-scale revival of old industrial clusters, it is often overlooked that new footloose industries do not need to establish ex ante local linkages in order to develop.

They often rely to a large extent on their own skills to create conditions for growth. For example, new environment-related industries are emerging in the Ruhr (the connection may be the solution of the pollution problem). In addition, there is little technological continuity between the textile machinery complex in New England of the 19th century and the current electronics cluster (Boschma and Lambooy, 1999).

4.2 War and Location of Firms

Unexpected political events (chances, accidents) such as wars, their start, intensity and length can not be predicted by everyone with a high degree of certitude. Nonetheless, wars decisively influence development, expansion, location, dislocation and spread of certain industries. There are numerous examples that support such arguments. For instance, as a late comer in the colonial era and because of post war(s) external sanctions, Germany had the 'incentives' (was forced by events) to produce various chemicals as substitutes for natural inputs that were not available either in colonies or through 'normal' trade. Self-sufficiency has often been of vital national importance. Germany's success was remarkable as the country developed world-leading chemical[13] and related industries such as pumps, sophisticated precision measurement and control instruments. Let us consider other examples.

- There was a recession in Seattle (Washington) after the First World War. The economy of the region was based on fishing, production of timber and ship/boat building. At about the same time demand for aircraft (made of wood) started to emerge. There were unemployed boat-builders and other inputs. Workers had talents in making wooden boats, they could easily make a fully covered boat (the body of an aeroplane), they also knew how to fix a propeller, which lead to the emergence of Boeing. The US was the country that took advantage of airmail on a large scale, large purchases of military aircraft and large demand for fast travel, which in turn provided domestic producers with early incentives to lower production and learning costs per aircraft as compared with foreign competitors.

---

[13] The German chemical industry was based on domestic deposits of salt and coal, as well as talents.

- The first commercially successful motor scooter, the Vespa, was produced by the Italian company Piaggio in 1946, although the idea for it was conceived during the Second World War.[14] During the war, Piaggio, at Pontandera, near Pisa, made aircraft engines. After RAF bombing destroyed the factories, warehouses and roads at the site, it became difficult and tiring to get around the site on foot. The company owner, Enrico Piaggio, asked one of his engineers, Corradino d'Ascanio to come up with a simple and economical two-wheel personal vehicle. D'Ascanio built the prototype using his imagination, the leftovers from small two-tact motors used to start the aircraft engines, aircraft wheels (note the shape of wheels on a Vespa when you next see one) and whatever else he could find in the warehouse (or what remained from it), such as metal sheets. It also incorporated a shield on each side to protect the rider's legs from injury. The prototype was ready within a few weeks and once in production, the Vespa became an immediate hit. It was extremely popular and fashionable in the 1950s and 1960s and was rediscovered by another generation in the 1990s because of increasing traffic congestion in cities.
- The Swiss chemical and heavy industry had certain benefits during the world wars. On the one hand, the German industry did not have access to the international market, hence the Swiss entrepreneurs filled the gap where they could. On the other hand, the Swiss benefited from the inflow of funds, talents and invalidation of German patents by the Allies.
- Caterpillar went from the US abroad during the Second World War in order to service machines that were used by the US Army. Following the War, the machinery that remained abroad had to be serviced. Hence, Caterpillar became an international company on a larger scale. Coca-Cola also followed the US Army during the Second World War to keep up the morale of the soldiers, and also remained abroad after it. Mars Bars were also distributed to armed forces all around the world during the War.[15]

---

[14] The first of many attempts to produce a small, economical runaround vehicle early in the 20th century resulted in the Auto-Ped. Introduced in New York in 1915, this looked like a child's scooter: it had no seat and there was a platform for the rider to stand on. A two-horsepower motor gave the Auto-Ped a maximum speed of 55 km/h.

[15] In an attempt to eliminate the textile waste during the Second World War, the US government reduced by one-tenth the amount of fabric allowed for women's

- Sialkot is a provincial town in the Punjab, Pakistan. It had a military garrison and a mission hospital during the British period a century ago. This created a demand for repair and, later on, production of surgical instruments, tennis rackets and footballs. The area had had a local tradition of producing swords and daggers for several centuries. When the military technology changed, the need for surgical instruments from the local hospital provided demand for sharp scalpels. Later on, around the Second World War, the supply of surgical instruments was necessary for the war efforts. Technology and experts were brought from Britain in order to support the production of those goods. Currently, a core of around 300 family-run firms (almost all have less than 20 employees) in Sialkot produce a range of 2,000 surgical instruments. They are, together with firms in Germany, major world exporters of surgical instruments. As Sialkot has no airport and as it is located over 1,500 km from the nearest sea port, a private self-help action created the Sialkot Dry Port Trust which brought 'the port to Sialkot'. The Trust offers a range of collective services such as customs clearance, warehousing and transport. The success of this, as well as all other clusters is based on two factors. First, the demand driven approach and, second, competition based on collective efficiency. However, not all is ideal in Sialkot. Infrastructure is still rather undeveloped. Power supply is inadequate, communications are poor and roads are covered with ankle deep mud during the monsoon season. Health and safety standards are insufficient and child labour is a serious problem in Sialkot's football making industry (Nadvi, 1998).
- Italian motor car racing companies such as Alfa Romeo, Ferrari and Lancia dominated the market in the period immediately after the Second World War. Within several years, however, a cluster of small firms from around Oxford became another dominant world player. There were several fortuitous events that prompted this evolution. First, there was a huge surplus of abandoned airfields in southern England after the War. Second, Mercedes withdrew from motor racing in 1955 after an accident in Le Mans in which 183 spectators were either killed or injured. This left room for the British racing car builders. Third, large and vertically integrated

swimwear. The chain of events that resulted in the ever decreasing amount of material necessary for the bikini was set in motion.

manufacturers such as Ferrari and Porsche built cars for their own racing teams, while the British were selling cars to everyone that wanted to buy them. Even though the British were not winning races, they dominated the staring grids with the number of cars. Fourth was the ban on cigarette advertising on TV in Britain in 1965. Tobacco companies became sponsors of motor racing with vast sums of money in return for having their logos on the racing cars. Pinch and Henry (1999) argue that although the success of the British constructors may have been influenced by a few accidents, it was only to a small extent. Other more important causes such as accumulated knowledge, its circulation through the companies by the means of transfer of personnel, as well as skilled labour, are the origins of the British success. The British have a tradition of expertise in engines and lubricants, aerodynamics and composite materials. In particular, the national aerospace industry was bigger and more sophisticated after the War than the one in Italy. This could, according to Pinch and Henry, probably have encouraged the production of racing cars even without the Mercedes crash and without the money from cigarette manufacturers.

- Another example about the impact of war on the change in the spatial distribution of production deals with the end of 'Cold War' around 1990. Huge defence cuts hit hard the military aerospace cluster in southern California.

4.3 CLUSTERS

Industrial clusters often determine what a country exports. Their success often establishes the competitive position of a country's goods and services on international market. Prior to the Industrial Revolution high transport costs splintered production in many units throughout space. The Industrial revolution reduced costs of transport, but brought high fixed costs that contributed to the development of new and expansion of the existing agglomerations.

A promising point of departure for the analysis of clusters is to consider two basic forces which, through their tension and interplay, influence the spatial distribution (concentration or spread) of firms. They are centripetal and centrifugal forces that also assist to explain the agglomeration and dispersion forces of the 'core-periphery'[16] development model.

- *Centripetal forces* promote agglomeration. They concentrate production and employment in specific geographical areas. These 'snowball' or herding forces include: economies of scale, forward and backward linkages in production, trade costs, increasing returns in transport, concentration of firms and consumers, existence of suppliers, limited spread of information and embodied knowledge, as well as thick labour market (especially for certain skills so that employers can find workers and workers can find jobs). Centripetal forces take the production system towards the equilibrium.
- *Centrifugal forces* push the other way and test if the equilibrium is stable. These dispersion (comparative advantage) forces discourage further spatial concentration of business. They favour a geographical spread of firms and include factor immobility, regional or international wage differentials, relative height of land rents, competition for factors and consumers, commuting costs, pollution, congestion, traffic accidents, crime, infectious and other diseases, sewage and waste disposal.

The final result depends on the balance between these two forces, on what factors are mobile and what immobile, on barriers to the reallocation of resources, on demand and its change and on public policy. In essence, three outcomes are possible. First, economic activity may spread so that each region becomes specialised in certain activity. This type of clustering does not mean polarisation as is exemplified in North America. The US economy is less geographically polarised than Europe. Second, activity may agglomerate in core regions leaving others without production potentials and without people. Finally, a long run polarisation may split the country or an economic grouping into advanced regions with high incomes and low unemployment and depressed regions with low income and high unemployment (Braunerhjelm *et al.*, 2000, pp. 29-30).

A concentration of functionally related business activity within a relatively small area (agglomeration; 'thick' market effects; benefits of co-

---

[16] A core region may be taken to mean the one that has capabilities and potentials to create, attract and employ resources and ideas. A periphery region may be taken to be the one that has the economic path determined chiefly by the developments in the core region(s).

location; and non-ergodicity) provides firms with collective gains that would not be available if the firms operated in a remote place. These shared benefits or externalities are different from the ones that are created within and available to a single firm. In essence, clusters create economies that are external to individual firms, but internal to a network of firms in a cluster, which are exchanged and enriched in a non-market way. Hence, a great deal of individual firm's competitive advantage is outside it, but inside the location where it operates.

A firm locates in an area where there are firms from the same or related industry (in a cluster) because:

- it has production links with other firms,
- it may benefit from the already existing pool of suppliers,
- there are services such as finance, information, consulting and maintenance,
- there may be a pool of trained and experienced labour,
- firms may reduce cost of transport,
- there may be a concentration of consumers (proximity to the major growing markets is often the most important reason for the selection of a particular location) and
- they may jointly negotiate contracts with transporters and organize export promotion boards and the like.

Manchester (England) in the 19th century provides the example of such type of cluster specializing in textile manufacturing. Subsequently, the manufacturing of looms and their reparation; bleaching, dying and finishing facilities also located there. In the course of time, the town set up a technical college in order to train people for the manufacture of machinery, textile design and other skills related to the local industry. All this was supported by marketing organizations such as the Cotton Exchange (Smith, 1981, pp. 60-1). A similar story can be told for Reutlingen in Germany. However, even the most recent industries rely on the 'old rule' of geographical concentration (clustering). That is why there is a Silicon Valley in California or Route 128 in Boston (because of the existence of the best universities in the vicinity).

A more recent example of similar developments in the manufacturing of surgical instruments and certain sports goods can be found in the town of Sialkot (Pakistan). This town is the leading world spot for exports of surgical instruments and hand-sawn balls for football. The success of this, as well as of all other clusters is based on two factors. First, demand driven approach and, second, competition based on collective efficiency (Schmitz, 1998, p. 6). An example of a joint action can be found in the surgical-instruments manufacturing cluster the Tuttlingen (Germany). The cluster produced joint publications on various topics of common interest. They include booklets on: quality requirements in the surgical-instruments-making industry; guide on how to use correctly the instruments; and a guide which gives the customer arriving in Tuttlingen the list and profile of firms that produce surgical instruments.

Technical advances in transportation, information technology, organisation and control of production and distribution reduce production time and costs. They 'do away' with distance. 'Globalisation' (integrated international production) creates possibilities to disperse production and ownership. In such circumstances already established spots face tougher times anchoring income-generating activities. At the same time, strong centripetal forces make certain spots remain 'sticky places in slippery space' (Markusen, 1996, p. 293). Spatial barriers for the location of businesses are becoming less important, but capital is more sensitive to the choice of location.

Up until the 1960s it seemed to be more efficient to move people to jobs by migration. The footloose element of many modern industries supports production in relatively small and flexible units. Hence, there is an arbitrary and uncertain element (multiple equilibria) in the location of firms that have footloose industrial character. Locations that are close to consumers save in transport costs of final output, while other locations may save in the cost of production. Due to costs of inputs, economies of scale and forwarding outlays, one business may favour peripheral locations, while for another a preference may be for locations nearest to the consumers.

A cluster is a relatively large group (a critical mass) and system of formal and informal functionally related specialised firms, knowledge, skills and competences, as well as specialised institutions (standards-setting bodies, schools, universities, research institutes, trade associations), in a particular geographical location. This functional relation among firms may be downstream (suppliers), horizontal (competitors and collaborators), upstream (clients) and/or through the circulation of accumulated knowledge, skills and competences by means of turnover of personnel.

Clusters, as spatially limited business incubators, are a part of the new industrial order named alliance capitalism in which continuous collaboration and networking with related knowledge and experience-rich firms are sources of competitiveness. It is also associated with the complex and dynamic 'new economy' based on knowledge and continuous innovation, as firms that operate in clusters are usually innovative. In addition, a vibrant dialogue is continuously taking place among all players in a cluster. The reason why this view fails to define a clear geographical boundary for a cluster is because the structure of a cluster may change over time. It does not refer either to the specific industrial boundary of a cluster, as this may overlook the complex relationship among different industries that support each other's competitiveness.

Agglomeration and the spatial clustering of firms and industries are motivated by efficiency considerations within a network. They are based on economies of scale in production and transportation, as well as on transaction costs. For example, the Massachusetts General Hospital in Boston is among the largest in the world in terms of R&D funds. Industrial managers come to the R&D Department of the Hospital because all the specialists and all the needed knowledge is 'within 20 minutes walking' (Lambooy, 1997, p. 298). This cluster of more than 400 firms linked to medical devices is invisible as it is concealed in business categories such as electronic equipment and plastics products.

Agglomeration does not apply only to private businesses. Because of the complexity of action and need for a fast response to changing and uncertain events, Simon Jenkins wrote that 'Britain is a centralised state. Two thirds of the top 100 powerful people in Britain work within 300ft of the Prime Minister and Chancellor of the Exchequer' (*The Times*, 11 December 2002).

Marshall (1890) considered the issue of why it is beneficial for producers from the same industry to be located together. He offered three basic reasons for the producers to concentrate (to form a cluster). These are:

- *Knowledge spillovers*: proximity eases exchange and spread of information.
- Advantages of *'thick markets' for specialised skills*: firms may easily find the necessary labour and workers may get promotion or work if the current employer does poorly. There is no need to create the human capital from scratch. The 'mysteries of trade' (craft secrets) are no mysteries at all as they are 'in the air' and children learn many of them unconsciously. Knowledge, experience and values are 'stored'. In addition, tacit knowledge and shared culture of beliefs and practices is difficult to transfer without labour mobility.
- Backward and forward *linkages* associated with large markets: links may clarify and explain a part of the concentration story only if there are economies of scale. Otherwise, a firm would set up a

separate production unit to serve each distinct market. A concentrated industry provides market for specialised local suppliers of components, as well as private and public suppliers of various services (institutional thickness).

These economies, external to individual firms in a cluster, but internal to a network of firms in a cluster, are essential, but not sufficient to explain the basic reason for the strength of firms in a cluster. Conscientiously pursued joint action and horizontal and vertical cooperation by firms in a cluster (sharing equipment, developing a new product, various consortia) enhance collective efficiency and improve the competitive advantage of the participating firms. When there is a problem (market failure), it can be resolved by government intervention and/or by private self-help (as was the case in Sialkot, Pakistan)[17] (Schmitz, 1999, pp. 468-70). However, relations between firms in a cluster may take different forms. Take a look, for example, at shoe producing clusters in Italy and Mexico. While cooperation is more common in Italy, market rules prevail in Mexico.

There are, however, additional reasons for the spatial clustering of firms and industries. They include the following:

- Owing to the changed situation in competition and technology, the past arm's-length and hierarchical organisation of a firm can be replaced by a flexible network of business organisation in a cluster. Inter-firm competition is based on innovation.
- Firms may reduce transaction costs.
- Presence of one firm/industry creates direct or indirect market for another firm/industry. One industry output is used exclusively as other industry's input (tyres and cars).
- Firms use common services (marketing, storage, accounting, repair, transport).
- Two industries use a common resource.
- Firms may create entry barriers.
- Labour markets of two unrelated industries may be complementary: one industry (metal or car assembly) uses male labour, while other(s) (textile or food processing) employs female labour.
- Firms use common social infrastructure (schools, health, roads).

[17] See section on the war and location of firms.

- The more there are the potential firms that can use infrastructure, the more likely that infrastructure would be built. Each user in a cluster assists other users in this situation, hence the fixed cost of an infrastructure project (such as educational and training centres, power plant, railway or airport) can be recovered and the project can come close to profitability. These are relatively standard projects, hence the government can be easily involved as the specific local knowledge is not always essential for the success.

The presence of a relatively large concentration of demanding consumers in an agglomeration, coupled with technologies with economies of scale, agglomeration forces can bring certain economic advantages through the interrelationship of functionally connected, as well as competing firms. Competition forces firms to employ state of the art technology, hence there are no low-technology industries, but only low-technology firms within various industries.

The clustering of firms selling identical goods (competitors) such as ice cream on the beach was thought to be welfare-inefficient from a social standpoint (Hotelling, 1929, p. 53). However, the clustering of firms often occurs in response to consumers' desires to make comparisons between goods (e.g., in shopping malls). They usually visit more than one store prior to making a purchase. Department stores often demand that certain space is made available in shopping malls to small shoe and apparel retailers. The reason is to assure clients that the offered goods are balanced by other competitive offers (i.e., that a minimum differentiation exists) for comparison. Clustering of *identical* firms can serve a socially-useful purpose because they lower transportation costs (Eaton and Lipsey, 1979, pp. 422-3). The same holds for clustering of *heterogeneous* firms. A rational consumer would connect purchasing activities such as search, purchase and transport. Multipurpose shopping assists in the lowering of shopping costs (Eaton and Lipsey, 1982, p. 58).

If the firms are similar, they seek comparable if not identical features for the spatial location of business. If this is true, then the outcome may be a cluster in such an industry. For example, the US film industry started a century ago in California, around Los Angeles. The concerned firms were similar. They were looking for comparable locational features such as dry weather and excellent daylight conditions. Although modern filming and lighting technology does not depend on natural light at all, the clustering of film and entertainment industry in California continued. Homogeneous initial needs of firms created the film cluster rather than input-output production relations. Hence, functional production links and agglomeration economies are not a necessary condition to create a cluster.

In spite of a few global TV stations such as the BBC or CNN and newspapers such as *The International Herald Tribune* or electronic media, one may easily find that most of the stories that the editors still publish or broadcast are indeed local. The proximity of firms in the same industry increases both the visibility of the course of action of competitors and the speed of the spread of information. 'Popular luncheon spots are patronized by executives from several companies, who eye each other and trade the latest gossip. Information flows with enormous speed' (Porter, 1990, p. 120). This 'cafeteria effect' breaks the spatial boundaries to information flow and gives incentives for the creation of matching improvements by other firms in the cluster. It also offers a partial confirmation that there is a spatial limit to knowledge spillovers. Information may be freely available notwithstanding distance, but the charge for the spread of embodied knowledge, in particular tacit, complex, changeable and 'sticky', goes up with the distance.[18]

The high speed of information diffusion is one of the major strengths of clusters. Entrepreneurs often prefer to enter or stay in a cluster even though they may be able to appropriate a higher return on their innovation elsewhere. The reason for the preference to stay in the cluster is that the firms are there not only providers of information, but also recipients (Schmitz, 1999, p. 475). In the fields where technology changes often, personal contact may be the preferred way of communication rather than the less timely sources such as professional journals, fairs and conferences. 'Human capital accumulation is a *social* activity, involving *groups* of people in a way that has no counterpart in the accumulation of physical capital' (Lucas, 1988, p. 19). This all supports progress in technology (creation of knowledge).

Personal contacts and informality are essential for the exchange of tacit knowledge. '*Tacit knowledge*, as opposed to *information*, … can only be transmitted informally, and typically demands direct and repeated contact. The role of tacit knowledge … is presumably the greatest during the early stages of the industry life cycle, before product standards have been

---

[18] Audretsch and Feldman (1996) found evidence that the US industries in which new knowledge spillovers are relevant (semiconductors and computers in California; pharmaceuticals in New Jersey) have a greater propensity to cluster innovative activity, than industries where these spillovers are less important. Bottazzi and Peri (2002) reported that the benefits of R&D in generating innovation were extremely localised.

established and a dominant design has emerged' (Audretsch, 1998, p. 23).[19] 'Companies that have gone furthest towards linking their global operations electronically report an increase, not a decline in the face-to-face contact needed to keep the firms running well: with old methods of command in ruins, the social glue of personal relations matters more than ever' (*The Economist*, 30 July 1994, p. 11). Such a durable social network that shortens the learning curve, informality in contacts and local embeddedness are essential to identify user requirements, proper installation, operation and service of the product.[20] Therefore, operation of firms within clusters makes firms relatively less sensitive to local taxes. This provides the local authorities with opportunities to tax them more heavily than would otherwise be the case.

The principal key of success in clusters of related firms in northern Italy ('Padania') is their ultra specialisation and family run type of business. Relatives support each other in business so there is no need for supervision, they relentlessly upgrade skills and they have opportunities for invention. Common values and local consensus is preserved. This reduces the possibility for business sclerosis, so common in large, vertically organised firms. For example, in Lumezzane (near Brescia) which produces two thirds of the national output of bottle openers: one family is strictly specialised in the production of screws, other has expertise in covers, etc. A similar situation is in Cadore (near Austria) with the production of spectacles. In general, company strategy is friendly with fast changes, customised products and niche marketing.

A summary of properties of such industrial districts would include (Garofoli,
1991, p. 52):

- a high level of division of labour between the firms and closer input-output relations;

---

[19] Information are simple structured and unstructured data. Knowledge is the capability to process those data, to analyse and to evaluate them and, possibly, to deepen and to extend them. Tacit knowledge is something that is within a knowledgeable person, but something that one cannot put in a manual.

[20] Personal contacts, face-to-face communication, proximity and trust with a partner are emphasised by Henderson *et al.* (2001), Venables (2001, p. 24), Crafts and Venables (2001, p. 32), Porter (2000, p. 262), Gordon and McCann (2000, p. 520), Sternberg and Tamásy (1999, p. 374), Porter and Sölvell (1998, pp. 445-6) and Kleinknecht and ter Wengel (1998, pp. 645-6), but were well known also to Perroux (1955, p. 317 and 1961, p. 152).

- a high level of specialisation which stimulates accumulation of knowledge and introduction of new technologies;
- a high level of skills of workers as a result of a very long-term accumulation of knowledge at a local level;
- a large number of local competitors which leads to the adoption of 'trial and error behaviour' and fast imitation process;
- efficient local informal (and formal) system for the exchange of information; and
- an increased emphasis on face-to-face relations.

The existence of the following elements could also be added:

- entrepreneurs,
- innovators,
- financial institutions with venture capital and
- demanding clients.

The growing importance of intangible assets, particularly intellectual capital together with complexities and changeability of information and uncodified knowledge, increases the importance of knowledge externalities (spillovers) and frequent face-to-face contacts among the relevant players. They need to exchange uncodifiable knowledge, to be involved in interactive learning, to have feedback and suggestions, as well as to have a dialogue about risk and changing situation in the market and technology. Clear-cut, routine and simple activities based on codified and standardised knowledge can be managed and controlled from a distance. They can be easily located in regions with lower wages. However, successful handling of more elaborate activities still requires a high degree of exchange of information and face-to-face contacts.[21] This is highly important in complex activities with no or little codified knowledge and where market changes and uncertainty require a fast response (contracts are incomplete). 'Knowledge is the most important resource and learning is the most important process' (Pinch and Henry, 1999, p. 820).

Knowledge externalities are among the key reasons for the existence and success of clusters. Hence, clusters may also be seen as networks for information gathering, facts processing and network production places. 'Almost every internationally successful Italian industry has several if not

[21] Do you know someone that learned to cook a good French or a Chinese dish only by reading a cookbook?

hundreds of domestic competitors. Frequently, they are all located in one or two towns. ... Where domestic rivalry is absent Italian firms rarely succeed internationally' (Porter, 1990, p. 447). Toyota in Japan, for example, is cultivating suppliers in it's own 'back yard'. Toyota independent suppliers are on average 94 km away from its assembly plants. They make nine deliveries a day. By contrast in North America, GM's suppliers are on average 683 km away from plants they serve to which they make fewer than two deliveries a day. One of the results is that Toyota and its suppliers keep inventories that are a quarter of GM's.[22] While just in time delivery and logistics method may be technically possible, organisationally feasible and financially desirable for a firm, an area that asks for further research includes environmental and social costs of this type of logistics. The just in time delivery method is often linked with half loads and more transport journeys than are the more traditional delivery methods.[23]

The existence of competitors in the vicinity serves a useful business and social purpose. If one imagines a cluster in the shape of an input-output matrix for information, then the direct and indirect functional relations are 'diffused' through rows and columns. Competition increases productivity which is the key ingredient of prosperity. Firms do not chase every chance to ruin rivals. This is contrary to the standard story in every introductory economic textbook.[24] Every firm in a cluster perceives its survival, growth and success in terms of collective growth. These firms learn and prosper collectively. The learning process in a cluster is not only interactive, but also cumulative as it persists over time (once it exists it does not cease to exist, experience and discovery builds on experience and discovery). Turnover of labour, technical staff and management among these firms reinforces the transfer of tacit knowledge, cross-fertilising research, collective learning process and regional competitive advantage.

The underlying general operations within a cluster can be seen from another example. 'New York City's garment district, financial district, diamond district, advertising district and many more are as much intellectual

[22] *Fortune*, 8 December 1997, p. 43.

[23] There was an estimate that empty trucks were making about 60 billion kilometres in the EU at an approximate annual cost of €45 billion. A better organisation of transport could radically reduce these figures (*The European Voice*, 29 January 1998, p. 15).

[24] Even though Siemens is a dominant firm in the Munich high technology cluster, it does not threaten or absorb SMEs in the cluster, but rather develops ties with SMEs that are characterised by collaboration (Sternberg and Tamásy, 1999, p. 375).

centers as is Columbia or New York University. The specific ideas exchanged in these centers differ, of course, from those exchanged in academic circles, but the process is much the same. To an outsider, it even *looks* the same: A collection of people in similar activities, each emphasizing his own originality and uniqueness' (Lucas, 1988, p. 38). Continuous and straight dealings among players allow tacit and accumulated knowledge to be exchanged within a network of players. Social closeness in such cases may be equally, if not more, relevant than the geographical proximity.

Established locations can be vulnerable to 'technological lock-in' in certain cases. New ideas may need new space. 'When IBM developed its own personal computer, the company located its fledgling PC capacity in Boca Ratton, Florida, way outside of the manufacturing agglomeration in the North-east Corridor' (Audretsch, 1998, p. 24). This is an example of a bifurcation point. In addition, certain industrial regions may become victims of own past success. Institutional sclerosis, vested interests of large firms, labour unions and public authorities may oppose changes and adjustment to new circumstances. For example, the German Ruhr region was led into the 'trap of rigid specialisation' (Grabher, 1993, p. 275). The Belgian Walloon region is in the same situation. However, it is sometimes overlooked that in certain cases new footloose industries often create own conditions for growth. For example, new environment-related industries are emerging in the Ruhr (the connection may be the solution of the pollution problem). In addition, there is little technological continuity between the textile machinery complex in New England of the 19th century and the current electronics cluster (Boschma and Lambooy, 1999, p. 394).

The existence of a good university or a research institute is not enough alone for the overall economic success of an area. During the period of central planning in the former Soviet Union, Akademgorodok (near Novosibirsk) was essentially a town full of research institutes financed by the Soviet Academy of Sciences. It remained an 'isolated island' as it has not developed functional links with industries. During the centrally planned period, the Soviet enterprises depended primarily on the respective ministries and the central plan.

Sophia-Antipolis was developed in vacant space at the end of 1960s in the south of France. It did not develop around an established university as was the case in Cambridge. A lot of time and effort, such as the establishment of the University of Nice, was necessary to create the necessary links among the high technology firms in the Sophia-Antipolis cluster. In general, it is hard to find any plan of action or best practice to promote a cluster that could have an instantly recognisable success.

However, there is a rare general agreement on one point. To have a commercial success, one needs to build on already existing competences in the target location.

The cluster of high technology firms around Cambridge (England) offers a different story. The common tacit code of behaviour among the high technology firms in the region includes trust and cooperation. The cluster is based on two local 'collective agents'. They are Cambridge University and consulting firms in R&D. In contrast to most other British universities which have formally regulated links with the industry, Cambridge has rather liberal rules governing such type of links. In fact, faculty members were allowed to work part time in the private sector. All this had a strong and positive spillover effect on the regional cluster of high technology firms.

There is also a view that 'clusters often emerge and begin to grow naturally. Government policy had little to do with the beginning of Silicon Valley or the concentration of mechanical firms around Modena, Italy. Once a cluster begins to form, however, government at all levels can play a role in reinforcing it. Perhaps the most beneficial way is through investments to create specialized factors, such as university technical institutes, training centres, data banks, and specialized infrastructure' (Porter, 1990, p. 655). In fact, many governments impeded the 'natural' development of clusters on behalf of regional policy and subsidised firms to locate in the areas with high unemployment and without supporting infrastructure (rather than to encourage migration of labour from these regions).

It was thought up until the 1960s that production costs were not sensitive to regional location. It does not come as a surprise that firms located in such areas became white elephants that demanded subsidies to continue operations later on. The importance of endogenous technological change became appreciated only in the following decades, so the policy of regional decentralisation became suspect (Bekar and Lipsey, 2001, p. 1). However, universities have always been established in cities. Children and students had to be assembled. Only relatively recently have universities become established in the countryside.

Governments and big TNCs often have nothing to do with the establishment of clusters (Silicon Valley, clusters in Italy, City of London financial district). They were created out of 'thin air'.[25] However,

---

[25] The emergence of a cluster may be based on a historical accident such as the existence of certain skills or raw materials or a crossroad. Its evolution may enter into the second phase with the agglomeration of firms and the arrival of externalities that may have cumulative features. Next step in the growth of a cluster may include creation of supporting bodies such as business associations

governments may easily support their growth through the provision of education, infrastructure, tax policy, public procurement, as well as through sponsoring of R&D.[26] All this ought to build on existing local specialties and competences, rather than to create entirely new ones. The private sector needs to lead the process, while the government needs to play a flexible catalytic role as one-size policy does not fit all clusters. There may not be a mechanical transfer of policy instruments from one cluster to another. Positive experiences from other clusters ought to provide more a source of inspiration and less a prescription for a general action.

Papageorgiou (1979) demonstrated that agglomerated firms can achieve higher aggregate profit, lower prices per unit of output and face increased demand than more dispersed firms. In addition, firms located in a cluster tended both to introduce more innovations and to grow faster than more isolated firms (Beaudry *et al.*, 2002, p. 191). Relative to the rest of the economy, clusters could have higher productivity, higher profitability, they may create more new jobs and new firms. On the cost side, land rents may

---

and knowledge related institutions (schools and research centres). The next stage includes the spread of the non-market relations. Firms and institutions create and maintain the spirit of strong non-market collaboration which is external to individual firms, but internal to the cluster. Such clusters may be highly specialised and may have success with their output on the market. However, they may easily become victims of their own success. They may get into a 'trap of rigid specialisation' as the final period in their life. They may be locked in their own technology, specialised output and spirit. If there is another, competing and new good, service or technology elsewhere, which is demanded, than the cluster may decline and demise.

[26] Public policy and administrative areas in which the authorities collect statistics are usually not equal to clusters. That is the reason why it is hard to determine the exact economic significance of clusters with a high degree of reliability.

increase in and around clusters and so can pollution and congestion. Labour costs can inflate, while institutions and specialisation may suffer from a path dependence and lock-in effect which may be unfriendly with adaptation to changes in technology that is not directly related to the specialisation in the cluster, but may easily alter the structure of general demand.

What are the implications for policy towards clusters? Well, new and successful clusters may appear. The examples of Ireland and costal region of China provide evidence for this statement. Economic integration and liberal treatment of trade and foreign investment may also assist. Many non-spatial policies such as education and training may have a stronger and more important impact than openly 'spatial' policies. A select list of clusters in the US, Italy and Germany is given in the Annex.

Chapter 5

CONCLUSION

Where a firm or an industry should locate is not a question with a straightforward answer. Rich nations fear the relocation of firms and industries to low-wage nations; poor nations worry that the production of goods and services will migrate to developed countries; while small countries are concerned that businesses will move to large countries.

At the time and age of 'globalisation' of business, one might expect the importance of firm location to be diminishing. Some argue that distance is dead in terms of production and business because of astonishing changes in communications and computers. 'Time zones and language groups, rather than mileage, will come to define distance' (Cairncross, 2001, p. 5). But this may be relevant only for certain manufacturing and services activities that are simple, routine and with codified knowledge. However, local proximity (clusters) of firms that produce similar, competing and/or related products together with supporting institutions still matters for complex activities, with no or lightly codified knowledge and where market changes and uncertainty require a rapid reaction. Economies of scale, activity-specific backward and forward linkages (indivisible production), accumulated knowledge, innovation, lock-in effects, existence of sophisticated customers and a fall in transportation costs play relevant roles in the protection of clusters and the absolute advantage of certain locations. 'Global' competitiveness often depends on highly concentrated 'local' knowledge, capabilities and a common tacit code of behaviour which can be found in a spatial concentration (a cluster) of firms. Hence, successful managers must often think in regional and act in local terms.

Availability of highly skilled and educated workers is becoming an increasingly important determinant for industrial location. This is reinforced by the limited spatial spillovers of knowledge, hence in certain industries 'local' clusters matter for the 'global' competitiveness of firms. National economic policies concerning investment, industrial change, R&D, mobility of people, skills and knowledge, investment in human capital (education) that develops and extends skills, experience and organisational competencies is crucial for the efficiency of the economy. Regional and social affairs also play a role as sometimes regional and social policies impede the development of clusters on behalf of equity considerations among national regions.

A century ago, even a half of a century ago economic theory looked at the location of firms and industries in a rather technical and deterministic way. Subjects and causes were separated from objects and effects, and everything ended up in equilibrium. Parts of modern spatial economics and the new geography of production consider the location of firms in an evolutionary way where the state of equilibrium is only temporary special case as everything is in an unstable organic process.

The new economic geography differs from the traditional model in several important dimensions. The new model makes a case that production specialisation in a given locality is not only based on certain comparative advantages, but rather on a self-reinforcing lock-in effect, path dependence, accumulated knowledge, agglomeration, clustering and linkages (indivisible production). In addition, while the traditional models reason that a reduction in trade costs among locations favours local specialisation, the new economic geography claims that the effect on local specialisation is ambiguous. The final outcome is industry specific and depends on the functional intra-industry production linkages, market structure, consumer preferences (homogeneity of tastes) and factor market (availability and mobility of factors and flexibility in prices). In general, the choice of location for a new investment or a new firm that produce tradable goods and services depends on a complicated interplay of at least three elements: factor intensity; transport intensity; and each in relation to the already established firms and their activities and (re)actions. Remote places do not necessarily need to be poor locations for firms as their remoteness is already reflected in their factor prices (Venables and Limão, 2002, pp. 260-1).

At the end, one may reason that there is an important lacuna in our understanding of spatial economics. It comes as no surprise that there are many disagreements and perhaps only four theoretical agreements:

- First, if one wants to start a new activity in a specific location, one has to build on already existing expertise and specialisation of that location.
- Second, if one wants to use policy intervention to influence the location of firms, this is most effective only very early in the process.
- Third, economies of scale and functional linkages in production have a certain impact on the location of firms and industries.
- Last, success or failure of a region or a policy sometimes depends on uncontrollable factors and events that are located outside regions themselves.[1]

The analysis of spatial economics depends on special assumptions. It is often a detective-type study and a collection of particular cases. Generality is often abandoned for discovery. This should not come as a surprise as spatial economics is simultaneously charged with some of the most difficult problems in economic theory: multiple equilibria, economies of scale, externalities, imperfect competition (which kind?), linkages and path dependence. Nonetheless, many useful things can be learned from exceptional cases. The examination of the issue is still elastic and highly suggestive (in particular how a historical accident may shape the production geography) than conclusive, convincing and general. A coherent theory of the subject is not yet in sight. However, there are various approaches that

[1] Coalmining regions weakened and declined when liquid fuels started to be used as principal sources of energy.

contribute to the raising of new questions and understanding of the issue. This leaves the topic subject of further theoretical and empirical analysis.[2]

[2] Topics for further research include: spillovers, externalities and linkages as they are so poorly understood; local interactions; monopolistic competition; cross-fertilisation with industrial organisation and urban economics, trade and growth; cost benefit analysis that can include linkages; services as research was mainly concentrated on the manufacturing sector; the speed of (exponential?) weakening of the effect of spillovers and information relative to distance especially in developing countries; and agglomeration and spread of innovative activities.

ANNEX

The production geography of the US is particularly interesting as it is a country without important internal borders and it is so big that it may serve as an example for economic comparison with an integrated Europe.[1] Even a superficial look at US production geography reveals a high concentration of industries. The implication is that the US clusters profit from large scale production for an almost homogenised large national market. For example, the following industrial clusters come to mind:

- aviation around Seattle
- finance on Wall Street
- insurance in Hartford (Connecticut)
- pharmaceuticals in central New Jersey
- medical equipment in Mineapolis
- electronics in the Silicon Valley and Boston's Route 128
- advertising on Madison Avenue in New York City
- optics related industries in Rochester (New York)
- cars around Detroit
- paints and coatings in Cleveland (Ohio)
- entertainment in California
- office furniture in western Michigan

---

[1] One has to be careful regarding comparisons between the current, post Second World War European integration and the evolution of integration in the US. To integrate the country, the American Civil War (1861-65) took the lives of around 620,000 persons in a nation of 35 million. (This loss would be comparable to a loss of 6.7 million people in the EU of 2003.) During this war, more persons died of disease and sickness such as dysentery, diarrhea, measles, malaria and typhoid than on the battlefield; the ratio was about 4:1.

- orthopaedic devices in Warsaw (Indiana)
- hosiery and home furnishings in North Carolina
- carpets in Dalton (Georgia)
- wine in Napa Valley (California)
- shoes in Massachusetts
- gambling in Las Vegas and Atlantic City

In Europe, production of knives is clustered in Solingen, watches in Geneva and the Swiss Jura, financial services in London, fashion garments and motorcycles in northern Italy, pleasure in Paris, flowers in Holland, sex/prostitution[2] in Amsterdam, carpets in Kortrijk (Belgium), but the European car industry has never created a cluster similar to Detroit.

Italy is an often quoted example of a country with distinct manufacturing clusters. A select group of those clusters include the following:[3]

- motorcycles in Bologna [2,370]
- electronics, mainly alarms for cars in Varese [100]
- jewellery in Valenza Po [1,400] (Alessandria); Vicenza [1,100]; Arezzo [1,300] (Florence)
- spectacles in Cadore [930] (Belluno)
- textiles and clothing in Sempione [3,900] (Varese)
- textiles around lake Como; Prato [8,481] (Florence); Olgiatese [2,614] (Varese); Biella [1,300] (Piedmont); Valdagno (Pisa)
- clothing in Val Vibrata [1,150] (Pescara); Empoli (Florence); Treviso
- female underwear in Castel Goffredo [280] (Mantova)
- silk in Comasco [2,600] (Como)
- wool in Biella
- knitwear in Carpi [2,054] (Modena)

2 This has always been an urban 'activity' because cities 'sell' anonymity and tolerance.

3 The list is based on data for 1996; if available the number of related firms in the cluster is given in square brackets; and a bigger city in the vicinity or province is given in 'normal' brackets. Source: "Quanti sono i distretti industriali in Italia?", *Newsletter Club dei Distretti Industriali* n° 9, Novembre 1998, Club dei distretti industriali Prato, p. 9.

- shoes in Fermo, Montegranaro, Porto Santelpidio, Sanbenedetto, San Benedetto del Trono (Ancona); Lucca, Santa Croce Sull'Arno [1,749] (Pisa); Ascoli [3,100]; Riviera del Brenta [886] (Padova)
- sports footwear in Montebelluna [623] (Treviso); Asolo (Treviso);
- tannery in Arzignano [600] (Vicenza) and Solofra (Naples)
- ceramic tiles in Sassuolo [199] (Bologna)
- marble in Apuo-Versiliese [1,161] (Carrara)
- taps and valves in Alto Cusio [300] (Novara)
- furniture in Brianza Comasca Milanese [6,500] (Milan); Cantù [7,200] (Milan); Alto Livenza [2,000] (Udine); Poggibonsi [1,294] (Siena); Bovolone-Cerea [3,000] (Verona)
- kitchens in Pesaro [1,200]
- chairs and tables in Udine [1,200]
- wood machinery in Rimini [1,345]
- agricultural machinery in Modena [100]
- foodstuffs in Parma [215]
- saucepans and valves in Lumezzane [1,008] (Brescia)
- packaging machinery in Bologna
- musical instruments in Castelfidardo [400] (Ancona)

Clusters in Germany:

- steel in Dortmund, Essen and Düsseldorf
- locksmith's products in Velbert
- cutlery in Solingen
- surgical instruments in Tuttlingen
- chemicals in Leverkusen, Frankfurt and Ludwigshafen
- jewellery in Pforzheim
- cars in Wolfsburg, Stuttgart, Munich, Ingolstadt, Neckarsulm and Regensburg
- machine tools in Stuttgart
- pens and pencils in Nuremberg
- printing presses in Heidelberg, Würzburg and Offenbach
- optics in Wetzlar
- tool-making in Remscheid

References

Altshuler, R., H. Grubert and T. Newlon (1998). 'Has U.S. investment abroad become more sensitive to tax rates?', NBER Working Paper No. 6383.

Arthur, B. (1989). 'Competing technologies, increasing returns, and lock-in by historical events', *Economic Journal*, pp. 116-131.

Arthur, B. (1990). 'Positive feedbacks in the economy', *Scientific American* (February), pp. 92-99.

Arthur, B. (1990a). 'Silicon Valley locational clusters: when do increasing returns imply monopoly', *Mathematical Social Sciences*, pp. 235-251.

Arthur, B. (1994a). 'Industrial location patterns and the importance of history', in *Increasing Returns and Path Dependence in the Economy* (ed. B. Arthur). Michigan: University of Michigan Press, pp. 49-67.

Arthur, B. (1994b). 'Urban systems and historical path dependence', in *Increasing Returns and Path Dependence in the Economy* (ed. B. Arthur). Michigan: Michigan University Press, pp. 99-110.

Audretsch, D. (1998). 'Agglomeration and the location of innovative activity', Oxford *Review of Economic Policy*, pp. 18-29.

Audretsch, D. and M. Feldman (1995). 'Innovative clusters and the industry life cycle', CEPR Discussion Paper No. 1161.

Auyang, S. (1998). Foundations of Complex-system Theories in Economics, Evolutionary Biology and Statistical Physics. Cambridge: Cambridge University Press.

Bair, J. and G. Gereffi (2001). 'Local clusters in global chains: the causes and consequences of export dynamism in Torreon's blue jeans industry', *World Development*, pp. 1885-1903.

Bartik, T. (1991). Who Benefits from State and Local Economic Development Policies? Kalamazoo: Upjohn Institute.

Beaudry, C., S. Breschi and P. Swann (2002). 'Clusters, innovation and growth', in *Multinational Firms* (eds J. Dunning and J. Mucchielli). London: Routledge, pp. 190-213.

Beckmann, M. (1999). Lectures on Location Theory. Berlin: Springer.

Bekar, C. and R. Lipsey (2001). 'Clusters and economic policy', Simon Fraser University, Vancouver, mimeo.

Bernstein, J. and D. Weinstein (2002). 'Do endowments predict the location of production? Evidence from national and international data', *Journal of International Economics*, pp. 55-76.

Blackhurst, R. and D. Henderson (1993). 'Regional integration arrangements, world integration and GATT', in *Regional Integration and the Global Trading System* (eds K. Anderson and R. Blackhurst). New York: Harvester Wheatsheaf, pp. 408-435.

Blonigen, B. (1997). 'Firm-specific assets and the link between exchange rates and foreign direct investment', *American Economic Review*, pp. 447-465.

Bottazzi, L. and G. Peri (2002). 'Innovation and spillovers in regions: evidence from European patent data', CEPR, Working Paper, No.215.

Brainard, W. and J. Tobin (1992). 'On the internationalization of portfolios', Oxford Economic Papers, pp. 533-565.

Brakman, S., H. Garretsen and M. Schramm (2002). 'The strategic bombing of German cities during World War II and its impact on city growth', CESifo Working Paper No. 808.

Braunerhjelm, P., R. Faini, V. Norman, F. Ruane and P. Seabright (2000). Integration and the Regions of Europe: How the Right Policies Can Prevent Polarization. London: CEPR.

Boschma, R. and J. Lambooy (1999). 'The prospects of an adjustment policy based on collective learning in old industrial regions', *GeoJournal*, pp. 391-399.

Cairncross, F. (2001). *The Death of Distance* 2.0. London: Texere.

Carlton, D. (1983). 'The location and employment choices of new firms: an econometric model with discrete and continuous endogenous variables', *Review of Economics and Statistics*, pp. 440-449.

Caves, R. (1996). Multinational Enterprise and Economic Analysis. Cambridge: Cambridge University Press.

Christaller, W. (1933). Die Zentralen Orte in Süddeutschland, Jena: Gustav Fischer. [Translated from German by C. Baskin Central Places in Southern Germany (1966), Englewood Cliffs: Prentice-Hall].

Crafts, N. and A. Venables (2001). 'Globalization in history: a geographical perspective', London School of Economics, Centre for Economic Performance.

David, P. (1984). 'High technology centers and the economics of locational tournaments', Stanford University, mimeo.

Davies, R. and D. Weinstein (2002). 'Bones, bombs and break points: the geography of economic activity', *American Economic Review*, pp. 1269-1289.

Dunning, J. (1988). Explaining International Production. London: Unwin Hyman.

Dunning, J. (1999). 'The eclectic paradigm as an envelope for economic and business theories of MNE activity', Discussion Paper No. 263, Department of Economics, University of Reading.

Eaton, C. and R. Lipsey (1976). 'The non-uniqueness of equilibrium in the Löschian location model', *American Economic Review*, pp. 77-93.

Eaton, C. and R. Lipsey (1979). 'Comparison shopping and the clustering of homogeneous firms', *Journal of Regional Science*, pp. 421-435.

Eaton, C. and R. Lipsey (1982). 'An economic theory of central places', *Economic Journal*, pp. 56-72.

Eaton, C. and R. Lipsey (1997). On the Foundations of Monopolistic Competition and Economic Geography. Cheltenham: Edward Elgar.

European Commission (1998). Foreign Direct Investment. London: Kogan Page.

Finger, J. and A. Yeats (1976). 'Effective protection by transportation costs and tariffs: a comparison of magnitudes', *Quarterly Journal of Economics*, pp. 169-176.

Fujita, M., P. Krugman and A. Venables (1999). The Spatial Economy. Cambridge: MIT Press.

Garofoli, G. (1991). 'Industrial districts: structure and transformation', in *Endogenous Development and Southern Europe* (ed. G. Garofoli). Aldershot: Avebury, pp. 49-60.

Gordon, I. and P. McCann (2000). 'Industrial clusters: complexes, agglomeration and/or social networks?', *Urban Studies*, pp. 513-532.

Grabher, G. (1993). 'The weakness of strong ties: the lock-in of regional development in the Ruhr area', in The Embedded Firm (ed. G. Grabher). *London: Routledge*, pp. 255-277.

Graham, E. (1978). 'Transatlantic investment by multinational firms: a rivalistic phenomenon?', *Journal of Post Keynesian Economics*, pp. 82-99.

Harris, C. (1954). 'The market as a factor in the localization of industry in the United States', *Annals of the Association of American Geographers*, pp. 315-348.

Henderson, J., Z. Shalizi and A. Venables (2001). 'Geography and development', *Journal of Economic Geography*, pp. 81-106.

Holmes, T. (1998). 'The effects of state policies on the location of manufacturing: evidence from state borders', *Journal of Political Economy*, pp. 667-705.

Hotelling, H. (1929). 'Stability in competition', *Economic Journal*, pp. 41-57.

Hymer, S., (1976). The International Operations of National Firms: A Study of Direct Foreign Investment. Boston: MIT Press.

Isard, W. (1954). 'Location theory and trade theory: short run analysis', *Quarterly Journal of Economics*, pp. 305-320.

Isard, W. (1956). Location and Space-Economy. Cambridge: Technology Press of MIT and London: Chapman & Hall.

Isard, W. (1996). Commonalities in Art, Science and Religion: An Evolutionary Perspective. Aldershot: Avebury.

Jovanović, M. (1998). International Economic Integration: Limits and Prospects. London: Routledge.

Jovanović, M. (2001). Geography of Production and Economic Integration. London: Routledge.

Jovanović, M. (2003). 'Spatial location of firms and industries: an overview of theory', Economia Internazionale, pp. 23-81.
http://papers.ssrn.com/sol3/papers.cfm?abstract_id=451800

Jovanović, M. (2003a). 'Local vs. global location of firms and industries', *Journal of Economic Integration*, pp. 60-104.
http://papers.ssrn.com/sol3/papers.cfm?abstract_id=394760#Paper%20 Download

Jovanović, M. (2005). *The Economics of European Integration*. Cheltenham: Edward Elgar.

Jovanović, M. (2006). *The Economics of International Integration*. Cheltenham: Edward Elgar.

Kleinknecht, A. and J. ter Wengel (1998). 'The myth of economic globalisation', Cambridge *Journal of Economics*, pp. 637-647.

Knickerboker, F. (1973). Oligopolistic Reaction and Multinational Enterprise. Boston: Harvard University.

Kravis, I. and R. Lipsey (1982). 'The location of overseas production and production for export by U.S. multinational firms', *Journal of International Economics*, pp. 201-223.

Krugman, P. (1979). 'Increasing returns, monopolistic competition and international trade', *Journal of International Economics*, pp. 469-479.

Krugman, P. (1980). 'Scale economies, product differentiation and the pattern of trade', *American Economic Review*, pp. 950-959.

Krugman, P. (1990). Rethinking International Trade. Cambridge MA: The MIT Press.

Krugman, P. (1991). 'History versus expectations', *Quarterly Journal of Economics*, pp. 651-667.

Krugman, P. (1992). Geography and Trade. Cambridge MA: The MIT Press.

Krugman, P. (1993). 'On the number and location of cities', *European Economic Review*, pp. 293-298.

Krugman, P. (1998). 'What's new about the new economic geography', *Oxford Review of Economic Policy*, pp. 7-17.

Krugman, P. (2000). 'Can America stay on top?', *Journal of Economic Perspectives*, pp. 169-175.

Lambooy, J. (1997). 'Knowledge production, organisation and agglomeration economies', *GeoJournal*, pp. 293-300.

Leamer, E. (1984). Sources of International Comparative Advantage. Cambridge: The MIT Press.

Leamer, E. and J. Levinsohn (1995). 'International trade theory: the evidence', in *Handbook of International Economics* (eds G. Grossman and K. Rogoff). Amsterdam: Elsevier, pp. 1339-1394.

Linder, S. (1961). An Essay on Trade and Transformation. Uppsala: Almquist & Wiksells.

Lipsey, R. (1992). An Introduction to Positive Economics. London: Weidenfeld and Nicolson.

Lösch, A. (1940). Die Räumliche Ordnung der Wirtschaft, Jena: Gustav Fischer [Translated from German by W. Woglom and W. Stolper, The Economics of Location (1973), New Haven: Yale University Press].

Lucas, R. (1988). 'On the mechanics of economic development', *Journal of Monetary Economics*, pp. 3-42.

Markusen, A. (1996). 'Sticky places in slippery space: a typology of industrial districts', *Economic Geography*, pp. 293-313.

Markusen, J. (1984). 'Multinationals, multi-plant economies and the gains from trade', *Journal of International Economics*, pp. 205-226.

Marshall, A. (1890). *Principles of Economics*. London: Macmillan.

Maurseth, P. and B. Verspagen (2002). 'Knowledge spillovers in Europe: a patent citations analysis', *Scandinavian Journal of Economics*, pp. 531-545.

Midelfart-Knarvik, K., H. Overman, S. Redding and A. Venables (2000). 'The location of European industry', *Economic Papers*, No. 142, European Commission.

Mody, A. and K. Srinivasan (1998). 'Japanese and U.S. firms as foreign investors: do they march to the same tune?', *Canadian Journal of Economics*, pp. 778-799.

Moses, L. (1958). 'Location and the theory of production', *Quarterly Journal of Economics*, pp. 259-272.

Murphy, K, A. Shleifer and R. Vishny (1989). 'Industrialization and the Big Push', *Journal of Political Economy*, pp.1003-1026.

Nadvi, K. (1998). 'International competitiveness and small firm clusters – evidence from Pakistan', *Small Enterprise Development*, pp. 12-24.

Ohlin, B. (1933). Interregional and International Trade. Cambridge: Harvard University Press.

Papageorgiou, G. (1979). 'Agglomeration', *Regional Science and Urban Economics*, pp. 41-59.

Penrose, E. (1952). 'Biological analogies in the theory of the firm', *American Economic Review*, pp. 804-819.

Perroux, F. (1950). 'Economic space: theory and applications', *Quarterly Journal of Economics*, pp. 89-104.

Peroux, F. (1955). 'Note sur la notion de, <pôle de croissance>', *Économie Appliqué*,
pp. 307-320.

Perroux, F. (1961). L'Économie du XXe Siècle. Paris: Presses Universitaires de France.

Pfann, G. and H. van Kranenburg (2002). 'Tax policy, location choices and market structure', Institute for the Study of Labor (IZA), Bonn, Discussion Paper No. 499.

Pinch, S. and N. Henry (1999). 'Paul Krugman's geographical economics, industrial clustering and the British motor sport industry', *Regional Studies*, pp. 815-827.

Porter, M. (1990). The Competitive Advantage of Nations. New York: The Free Press.

Porter, M. (2000). 'Locations, clusters and company strategy', in *The Oxford Handbook of Economic Geography* (eds G. Clark et al.). Oxford: Oxford University Press, pp. 253-274.

Porter, M. and Ö. Sölvell (1998). 'The role of geography in the process of innovation and the sustainable competitive advantage of firms', in *The Dynamic Firm* (eds A. Chandler et al.). Oxford: Oxford University Press, pp. 440-457.

Posner, M. (1961). 'International trade and technical change', *Oxford Economic Papers*, pp. 323-341.

Reuber, G. (1973). Private Foreign Investment in Development. Oxford: Clarendon Press.

Rugman, A. (2002). 'Multinational enterprises and the end of global strategy', in Multinational Firms (eds J. Dunning and J. Mucchielli). *London: Routledge*, pp. 3-17.

Rugman, A. and R. Hodgetts (2001). 'The end of global strategy', *European Management Journal*, pp. 333-343.

Sachs, J. (2000). 'Globalization and patterns of economic development', *Weltwirtschaftliches Archiv*, pp. 579-600.

Schmitz, H. (1998). 'Fostering collective efficiency', *Small Enterprise Development*, pp. 4-11.

Schmitz, H. (1999). 'Collective efficiency and increasing returns', *Cambridge Journal of Economics*, pp. 465-483.

Smith, D. (1981). *Industrial Location – An Economic Geographical Analysis*. New York: John Wiley.

Sternberg, R. and C. Tamásy (1999). 'Munich as Germany's no. 1 high technology region: empirical evidence, theoretical explanations and the role of small firm/large firm relations', *Regional Studies*, pp. 367-377.

UNCTAD (1993). World Investment Report: Transnational Corporations and Integrated International Production. New York: United Nations.

UNCTAD (1997). World Investment Report: Transnational Corporations, Market Structure and Competition Policy. United Nations: New York.

UNCTAD (2002). World Investment Report: Transnational Corporations and Export Competitiveness. United Nations: New York.

UNCTAD (2003). World Investment Report: FDI Policies for Development – National and International Perspectives. United Nations: New York.

Venables, A. (1996). 'Localization of industry and trade performance', *Oxford Review of Economic Policy*, pp. 52-60.

Venables, A. (2001). 'Geography and international inequalities: the impact of new technologies', London School of Economics, Centre for Economic Performance.

Venables, A. and N. Limão (2002). 'Geographical disadvantage: a Heckscher-Ohlin-von Thünen model of international specialisation', *Journal of International Economics*, pp. 239-263.

Vernon, R. (1966). 'International investment and international trade in the product cycle', *Quarterly Journal of Economics*, pp. 190-207.

von Thünen, J. (1826). Der Isolierte Staat in Beziehung auf Landtschaft und Nationalökonomie. Hamburg: Perthes. [Translated from German by C.

Wartenberg, von Thüunen's Isolated State (1966), Oxford: Pergamon Press].

Wasylenko, M. (1991). 'Empirical evidence on interregional business location decisions and the role of fiscal incentives in economic development', in *Industry Location and Public Policy* (eds H. Herzog and A. Schlottmann). Knoxville: The University of Tennessee Press, pp. 13-30.

Weber, A. (1909). Über den Standort der Industrien, Tübingen: J.C.B. Mohr [Translated from German by C. Friedrich, *Theory of the Location of Industries* (1962), Chicago: University of Chicago Press].

Wheeler, D. and A. Mody (1992). 'International investment location decisions: the case of U.S. firms', *Journal of International Economics*, pp. 57-76.

Yamawaki, H. (1993). 'Location decisions of Japanese multinational firms in European manufacturing industries', in *European Competitiveness* (ed. K. Hughes), pp. 11-28.

ACKNOWLEDGEMENTS

Je tiens à remercier tout particulièrement Marinette Payot qui m'a beaucoup aidé sans que je le sache. I have benefited from discussions with and intellectual capital of many friends and colleagues, but I owe special gratitude to Amedeo Amato, Lisa Borgatti, Ron Boschma, Gioacchino Garofoli, Birgit Hegge, Jovan Jovanović, Jong Eun Lee, Antonio Majocchi, Marina Rossi, Bertram Schefold and James Wiltshire. Christopher Smith edited the text. The views expressed are my own and do not reflect the position of the organisation for which I work.

INDEX

D

E

F

N

O

P

R

S

T

U

V

W